Anastasia
On Her Own

Books by Lois Lowry

Anastasia Krupnik

Anastasia Again!

Anastasia at Your Service

Anastasia Off Her Rocker

Anastasia on Her Own

Anastasia Has the Answers

Anastasia's Chosen Career

Anastasia at this Address

Anastasia, Absolutely

A Summer to Die

Find a Stranger, Say Goodbye

Autumn Street

Taking Care of Terrific

The One Hundredth Thing About Caroline

Us and Uncle Fraud

Anastasia On Her Own

Lois Lowry

Houghton Mifflin Harcourt
Boston New York

For information about permission to reproduce selections from this book,
write to trade.permissions@hmhco.com or to Permissions, Houghton Mifflin Harcourt
Publishing Company, 3 Park Avenue, 19th Floor, New York, New York, 10016.
www.hmhco.com

The text of this book is set in Adobe Garamond Pro.

The Library of Congress has cataloged the hardcover edition as follows:
Lowry, Lois.
Anastasia on her own.
Summary: Her family's new organized schedule for easy housekeeping makes
thirteen-year-old Anastasia confident that she can run the household while her
mother is out of town, until she hits unexpected complications.
[1. Family life—Fiction.] I. Title.
PZ7.L9673Ap 1985 [Fic] 84-22432

ISBN: 978-0-395-38133-5 hardcover
ISBN: 978-0-544-54027-9 paperback

Manufactured in the United States of America
DOC 10 9 8 7 6 5 4 3 2 1
4500571883

For Becky

Anastasia On Her Own

one

"It's starting to snow," Anastasia announced as she came through the back door. "It's really coming down. Maybe if it snows all night there won't be any school tomorrow—I hope, I hope."

She dropped her schoolbooks on the kitchen table with a thump. "What's for dinner?" she asked her mother. "Why are you just standing there with that sort of frown on your face? And your lips are green. Why are your lips green?"

Mrs. Krupnik sighed. She poked out her tongue, tasted her lips, and made a face. "It's ink," she said. "I was working on some book illustrations all afternoon, and I was using green ink. I can't seem to quit putting the tip of my brush in my mouth."

"It looks gross," Anastasia said cheerfully. "It makes you look like some science-fiction creature."

"Thanks a *lot*," said her mother crossly. "You really know how to make a person feel terrific, Anastasia." She rubbed her mouth with a damp dishtowel; then she stared at the smeared cloth. "*Great.* Now I've ruined a perfectly good towel."

"Yeah, but your lips look a little more normal. What's for dinner?" Anastasia asked again. "And why are you so grouchy?"

"I'm not grouchy. I'm perplexed." Mrs. Krupnik sat down in a kitchen chair and sighed again. "I'm perplexed because it's time to cook dinner, and I don't *know* what we're having for dinner. I forgot to take any meat out of the freezer."

Anastasia groaned. She took off her snowy parka and hung it on a hook in the back hall. "Again?" she asked. "You forgot to take meat out of the freezer yesterday and we had to have grilled cheese sandwiches for dinner. And the day before that, you—"

Her mother interrupted her. "I know. Chunky Soup. I just can't seem to get my act together when it comes to making dinner. I'm good at a lot of stuff:

illustrating, growing begonias, playing trucks with your brother, even matching up the socks when they come out of the dryer. And I'm a good mother, I guess. Would you say I'm a good mother?"

"Yeah. You're okay," Anastasia said, and opened the refrigerator door. She made a face. "Isn't there anything for a snack, even?"

"Saltines."

"Yuck." Anastasia went to the cupboard and took a saltine from the box. She looked at it apathetically and put it back. "Daphne's mother made chocolate chip cookies today. And Sonya's mother made brownies. I pigged out at both their houses on the way home from school. That's why I'm late. Why don't you ever make brownies?"

"I'm a lousy homemaker. I'm a good *cook;* but how can I cook something when it's all frozen solid? Why do I always forget to take things out of the freezer? And sometimes I forget to do the laundry, too. I bet your friends' mothers all remember to wash the clothes."

"Yeah, probably. Daphne likes her clothes dirty, though. She has a pair of jeans that haven't been washed in a year. They can stand up by themselves.

She hides them in her closet, standing up, so her mother won't wash them."

"Maybe that's what I should do. I should hide in a closet, standing up. Then no one would notice what a rotten housekeeper I am." Mrs. Krupnik stood up and went to the pantry.

Anastasia watched her disappear into the small room. "You're not really doing it, are you?" she called. "Hiding in there? Because I'll tell Dad. You can't trust me to keep a secret like that, Mom."

Her mother reappeared, holding a box. "No. If I ever disappear, if I ever go into hiding, it'll be in that big closet off the guest room, the one where the summer clothes are stored. I was just looking in the pantry for something we could have for dinner. What do you think about"—she read the label from the dusty box—"instant meatless enchiladas?"

"You want honesty, or politeness?"

"Honesty."

"Barf. That's what I think."

"Yeah, me too." Mrs. Krupnik put the box on the table and sank into the chair again. "Is it snowing hard? Is the driving terrible? Maybe your dad could go get some pizza."

Anastasia went to the window and rubbed a circle clear with the palm of her hand so that she could look out. "The street's still bare," she said. "Is Dad home yet? I'll go ask him."

Her mother nodded. "He's home early today. He's reading to Sam." She looked gloomily at the window where Anastasia's circle had filled in again with steam. "Now the window will be all smeared. And I never seem to get around to washing the windows. I am such a hopeless failure at housework, Anastasia. *Hopeless.* Maybe I should subscribe to *Good House-keeping.* Maybe that would help."

"Don't do anything drastic and irrevocable, Mom. Probably there are easier solutions. Dad and I will give it some thought. In the meantime: loaded, no anchovies?"

"And extra cheese," her mother said.

"You got it." Anastasia headed for the study to find her father.

All four Krupniks sat in the study, in front of a roaring fire in the fireplace, with a huge pizza on the big coffee table. Strings of cheese dangled from their chins. A Beethoven symphony played on the stereo.

Outside, the wind howled and a tree branch tapped against the side of the house.

"Isn't this great?" asked Anastasia's father. "Isn't this the best of all possible worlds? Don't you feel as if you have absolutely no problems on a cozy night like this?"

"I have a problem," Mrs. Krupnik said.

"I have a problem, too," Anastasia said.

"I have a big problem," Sam announced, with his mouth full. "Not enough mushrooms on my pizza."

Myron Krupnik sighed. "Well, I'm shot down again. Here, Sam. You can have some of my mushrooms." He scooped them off his pizza slice with his hand and deposited them on Sam's slice. "Now: Sam, you got a problem?"

"Nope," said Sam, chewing vigorously. "No problems."

"Anastasia?" her father asked. "What's your problem? You want my pepperoni? Am I going to get stuck with a naked pizza?"

"No, my pizza's fine. My problem has to do with school. English class in particular."

Her father grinned and stretched his long legs out toward the fire. "Well, I'm not an English professor for nothing. Ask me anything. You want the major themes in Shakespeare? A brief but scintillating history of Restoration drama? How about—"

"*Dad*. Don't go off on a whole big lecture. My problem is a personal one, and it has to do with Steve Harvey, and it just happened to take place in English class."

Sam giggled. "Anastasia loves Steve," he said. "Steve is Anastasia's boyfriend."

"Quit it," Anastasia said, and poked her brother. "Three-year-olds don't know anything about boyfriends and girlfriends."

"Kiss me, Steve," said Sam dramatically, and he made loud kissing noises in the air. A mushroom flew out of his mouth.

"QUIT IT!" Anastasia bellowed.

"Sam," ordered Mrs. Krupnik, "stop teasing your sister."

Sam plucked his lost mushroom from the couch, where it had landed, and popped it back into his mouth. He grinned.

"May I continue?" Anastasia asked sarcastically. Everyone, including Sam, nodded.

"Okay. Thank you. Now, as idiotic Sam pointed out, Steve Harvey is sort of my boyfriend."

"Excuse me for interrupting, Anastasia," said her mother, "but what exactly does that *mean?* Are you and Steve going steady, or what?"

"Mom," Anastasia explained, "you have to forget about all those obsolete terms from your youth. Nobody 'goes steady' anymore."

"Anastasia and Steve," Sam began in a singsong voice, "are going to get marri—"

"SAM!" roared his parents in unison.

"Sorry," Sam said, and went back to his pizza.

"It doesn't 'mean' anything," Anastasia tried to explain. "It's just that Steve and I are sort of a couple, that's all. Like Daphne and Eddie, and Sonya and Norman. When people think of me at school they think of Steve. They think: Anastasia and Steve. We're a pair."

"Well, okay," said her father. "I guess we can understand that. But what happened in English class?"

"The teacher was talking about poetry. And she was talking about this really boring stuff, about meter and rhyme, and—"

"That's not boring!" said her father. "Anastasia, how can you say that's boring? Are you forgetting who your old man is?"

Anastasia cringed. She *had* forgotten, for a moment, that her father was a well-known poet. She glanced guiltily at the several volumes of his poetry, there on the shelves of the study. One of those books was even dedicated to her.

"Well, okay, I'm sorry, Dad. I know it's not boring to you. But to seventh-graders, it's kind of boring. I'm really sorry, but that's true."

Her father lit his pipe. "All right," he said. "Come to think of it, I guess I was bored by poetry in the seventh grade too. Go on."

"Well, she was talking about *feet*. I bet you didn't even know that, Dad, that poetry has feet?"

Sam giggled. He wiggled his toes, in their little blue socks, ostentatiously. "Feet," he murmured. "Feet feet feet."

"SAM!"

"Sorry," Sam said, and gave one last wiggle.

"Of course I know that, Anastasia. What do you think I teach at Harvard, nursery rhymes? I spend entire lectures on metrics. Did your teacher talk about the dactyl, and the spondee, and—"

"Yeah," said Anastasia gloomily. "You're getting warm. Keep going."

Her father chewed on his pipe, puzzled. "The trochaic foot, and the anapest—"

"That's it!" Anastasia wailed. "You see what I mean?"

Her parents were silent. Even Sam was silent. They all looked mystified.

"The *instant* the teacher said that last one—ugh, I can hardly bear to say it—"

"Anapest," her father repeated. "Da-da-DUM. That's an anapestic foot."

"GROSS," said Anastasia. "Steve Harvey, that rat, that absolute *rat*, called out, right in class: 'Anapestic Krupnik!' I wanted to die."

Her father chuckled. "Well, I can see that there's a certain similarity of sound. He was pretty clever to pick up on that."

"And all the rest of the day," Anastasia went on, "everyone was calling me that. Anapest, that's what they were calling me."

Sam opened his mouth. His mother glared at him. He closed his mouth again.

"And last *week*—last week it was science class, for Pete's sake. We had this gross word in science class; I bet you don't even know what it means."

"What *what* means?" asked her mother. "I bet I know. I was pretty good in science."

"I don't even want to say it," Anastasia muttered. "It's so gross."

"Whisper it," her father suggested.

Anastasia said something under her breath.

"Whisper it louder, please."

She whispered it a little louder.

"ANASTAMOSIS!" Sam repeated loudly.

Anastasia didn't even yell at her brother. She huddled miserably on the couch. "They called me that last week," she said. "Anastamosis Krupnik. And it was Steve who started it."

"It sounds to me," Mrs. Krupnik suggested, "as if Steve is paying a lot of attention to you."

"Yeah," Anastasia acknowledged. "But it's humiliating."

"Anastasia?" Sam said. "Can I say something? I want to say something really helpful."

"Okay."

"You could call *Steve* something bad. Then he'd know how it feels."

"Like what?"

Sam put his thumb in his mouth and thought.

Finally he took his thumb out. "Dog doo," he suggested.

Anastasia broke up. Laughing, she reached for the last cold slice of pizza. "Thanks, Sam," she said. "But I think I need something more mature."

Dr. Krupnik stood up and poked the logs in the fire. He turned a large one over so that its red, glowing underside was exposed. "Actually," he said, "I think your problem is solved, Anastasia. Has your teacher finished with the discussion of metrics?"

"Yeah. I think so. We have a quiz tomorrow, and then after that we start reading *Lorna Doone.*"

"Well, I don't think you're going to encounter any more words that resemble your name. There couldn't possibly be any others. It was just a fluke, that those two—*anapest* and—what was the other one?"

"*Anastamosis,*" Anastasia mumbled reluctantly.

"What *does* that mean, Katherine?" Dr. Krupnik asked his wife.

She shook her head. "Beats me," she said.

"Anastasia?" he asked.

She groaned. "It's something disgusting," she said. "I forget exactly. But it's in the intestines."

"At nursery school," Sam announced, "we have a Visible Man, and you can see his insides. And my favorite part of the Visible Man is the intestines. I call them the *guts*."

"*SAM,*" everyone bellowed.

"Sorry," Sam said, for the third time.

"Katherine," Dr. Krupnik said over coffee, "we all got sidetracked discussing Anastasia's problem, and we forgot to ask what yours was."

Mrs. Krupnik took out her knitting. "Oh, it's just my usual problem. It's why we had pizza for dinner, and no dessert. I'm the world's worst housekeeper."

"I wouldn't call you the world's worst, Mom," Anastasia said. "I read in the newspaper about a woman who died in New Orleans, and she was about ninety, and in her house they found forty cats, and a whole kitchen filled with dirty dishes, stacked practically to the ceiling, and first they tried to clean and fumigate her house, but eventually they just gave up and knocked the whole house down with a bulldozer, it was that bad."

"You're very comforting, Anastasia," said her mother tersely. "I am truly pleased to hear that you don't think I'm quite as bad as the woman in New Orleans. Bear in mind, though, that I am not yet ninety."

"Did they take the cats out first?" asked Sam, with his eyes wide. "Or did the cats get mashed by the bulldozer?"

"The Humane Society took the cats and found homes for them," Anastasia reassured him.

"Organization," said Dr. Krupnik.

"Well, of course it's an organization, Dad," said Anastasia. "Everybody knows the Humane Society's an organization. I didn't think I had to explain that."

"No, no; I meant that *organization* is your mother's problem. She's not very well organized."

"I know that, Myron," said Mrs. Krupnik, with a sigh. "I'm organized in my work, though. I always get illustrating jobs done on time; nobody's ever complained."

"That proves that you are *capable* of good organization. What you need to do is make a list."

Mrs. Krupnik groaned and began to knit very fast. "I hate lists," she said.

"I love lists," said Dr. Krupnik. He leaned back and puffed on his pipe, thinking happily about lists.

"I love lists too," said Anastasia. Her bedroom upstairs was absolutely filled with lists.

They all looked at Sam to see if he hated or loved lists. But Sam had curled up with his head on a cushion of the couch. His eyes were closed, and his thumb was in his mouth.

"See?" said Mrs. Krupnik suddenly, and she put her knitting down. "SEE? It's nine o'clock, for heaven's sake. And I completely forgot to put Sam to bed. You see what a disorganized person I am? I'm *hopeless!*"

"Anastasia," said her father, "while Mom takes Sam upstairs, you and I are going to sit here in the study, in a very organized fashion, and we're going to make a housekeeping list. Is that okay with you, Katherine?"

Mrs. Krupnik had picked up sleeping Sam. "Fine," she said.

Anastasia went to the desk and got some paper and two pens. "I love making lists," she said again. "And I sure hope it keeps snowing and school is canceled tomorrow, because if not, I'm going to flunk that quiz on poetry feet for sure."

>< >< ><

"Now," said Dr. Krupnik, holding his pen poised over a blank sheet of paper, "the thing to do is to divide the day into segments. Each one should be an hour, starting at—"

"Hold it," Anastasia said. "We need a title first."

"Easy. 'Katherine Krupnik's Housekeeping List.' That's the title. Now, if we divide the day—"

"Hold it. I hate that title."

"Why? What's wrong with it?"

"It's sexist. Didn't we once all agree that we would share the housekeeping? We each have a night to do the dishes. Why all of a sudden is it 'Katherine Krupnik's Housekeeping List'? I think that's very antifeminist," said Anastasia.

Her father frowned. "You sound like some of my students," he said. "But you're right, I guess. New title: 'Krupnik Family Nonsexist Housekeeping List.'" He wrote it down.

"Make that 'Schedule' instead of 'List.' Mom hates lists."

He made the change. "Now," he said, "starting at seven a.m., we all get up."

"Hold it. I don't get up at seven a.m."

Anastasia's father looked at her in astonishment.

"Every morning, at seven a.m., just as I'm going into the bathroom to shave, I hear your mother stand at the foot of the stairs to the third floor and call, 'Time to get up, Anastasia!'"

"What do you mean, 'shave'? You don't shave—you have a beard."

Her father stroked his beard. "People with beards shave. I shave my *neck*. What do you mean, you don't get up?"

Anastasia squirmed uncomfortably. "Well, I sort of hear Mom at seven. But I don't *really* hear her till seven-thirty."

"You mean she calls you again at seven-thirty?"

"Yeah," Anastasia admitted. "At seven-thirty she yells, 'If you don't get your buns out of that bed this minute, you're going to be late for school!' Then I get up."

"Should we put that on the schedule?"

Anastasia frowned. "No," she said, finally. "I'll try to get up at seven."

Her father wrote in the seven a.m. activities. "Now we'll move ahead to eight, when you and Sam and I all leave."

"Hold it."

"What?"

"Well, she has to help Sam get dressed, and she cooks breakfast. And when she remembers it, she gathers up the dirty clothes and takes them downstairs to the washing machine."

"How does she have time to do all that?" asked Dr. Krupnik.

Anastasia shrugged. "I don't know. I have enough trouble getting my buns out of the bed."

"We should help more."

"Yeah."

Dr. Krupnik wrote some things down.

"Okay," he said, "now it's eight o'clock and we're all gone and she's home alone. What does she do then?"

"That's when she forgets to take something out of the freezer for dinner. She starts working, in the studio, and she loses track of everything else."

"She won't," he said with satisfaction, "once she has this schedule in front of her."

He wrote some more things down.

"Hold it," said Anastasia. "You forgot the beds. She makes Sam's bed, and I guess she makes your bed, unless you do. Do you ever make your bed?"

"No," Dr. Krupnik said guiltily. "I guess I should. Do you make your bed?"

"Well, I'm supposed to. Sometimes I do."

"I'll put that in," he said, and wrote it down. "Okay. Now she can go to work in the studio. She can work the rest of the morning. I'll write in a coffee break, too."

"Hold it. What about the laundry?"

"Can't she do that on her coffee break?" Dr. Krupnik asked.

"That's a pretty crummy coffee break, if you ask me."

"Yeah. Well, what if she does the laundry at noon?"

"But that's when Sam comes home, and she fixes their lunch, and sometimes she and Sam go out then to do the shopping."

Dr. Krupnik chewed on the end of the pen. "How about this? If she puts the clothes in the washing machine after lunch, then the clothes will wash while they're out shopping."

"Okay. And then she can put them in the dryer when she gets home."

He wrote that down. "Hey," he said, "we're up to two p.m. already."

"Sam takes a nap then, and Mom works some more in the studio. After Sam wakes up, she plays with him."

"This is great," said Dr. Krupnik. "This is so organized, it's fantastic. How do you like this idea? When Sam wakes up, he can help her take the clothes out of the dryer. *Then* they can play, and look — by then it's four p.m. By then you're coming home from school, right?"

"Right," said Anastasia, "unless I stay late for something. Right about four p.m. is when she sinks into a depression."

"Why does she do that?"

"Because she realizes she forgot to defrost something for dinner."

"Oh. Well, we took care of that, because we wrote it into the schedule in the morning. Now she cooks dinner, and you and I come home, and we all eat —"

"I set the table," Anastasia pointed out.

"Right. And then we each take turns doing the dishes, and then at eight p.m. she gives Sam a bath, and —"

"You do that sometimes."

"Well, okay, somebody gives Sam a bath, and puts

him to bed, and then we all just relax. The workday is over."

"Hold it."

"What did I forget?"

"When does she vacuum? And wash windows and stuff?"

Dr. Krupnik made a face. Then, after a moment, he brightened. "Saturdays," he said.

With a flourish he made a note about Saturdays, and the schedule was finished.

"Housekeeping is simple," Dr. Krupnik said.

"Yeah," said Anastasia. "Any moron could do it. All you need is a schedule."

Krupnik Family Nonsexist Housekeeping Schedule

7:00 A.M.   Everyone gets up.
             Anastasia makes bed.
             Myron makes bed.
             Katherine makes Sam's bed.
             Katherine helps Sam dress.
             Katherine makes breakfast.
             Everyone eats.

8:00 A.M.   Katherine takes food out of freezer.
             Myron and Anastasia leave for school.
             Nursery school carpool picks up Sam.
             Katherine goes to work in the studio.

10:00 A.M.   Katherine's coffee break.

NOON   Carpool brings Sam home.
             Katherine and Sam have lunch.

1:00 P.M.   Clothes into washing machine.
             Sam and Katherine do shopping.

2:00 P.M.   Clothes into dryer.
             Sam takes nap.
             Katherine works in studio.

3:00 P.M.   Sam and Katherine fold clean laundry.
             They play.

4:00 P.M.   Katherine starts dinner.
             Anastasia comes home from school.

5:00 P.M.   Myron gets home.

6:00 P.M.   Anastasia sets table.
             Everyone eats.

7:00 P.M.   Katherine, Myron, or Anastasia does dishes,
             depending on whose turn.

8:00 P.M.   Someone bathes Sam and puts him to bed.

*** vacuuming, window-washing, etc., on Saturdays

*T*hwack, *thwack, thwack*. Down the long school hallway, one locker door after another slammed shut with a metallic sound. Anastasia zipped up her parka, sorted out her books, collected the ones she needed for homework, and pulled on her knitted ski hat. At the locker next to hers, Sonya Isaacson muttered, "I really flubbed that English quiz. My parents are going to be mad."

"Me too," Anastasia said. "I thought school would be called off today because of the snow. So I didn't even study. I think I got all the true-false, though."

"Quick, turn around," Sonya whispered suddenly. "Here comes Norman. Pretend you don't see him."

Automatically Anastasia obeyed, turning sideways toward her locker as if she needed more books. Sonya did the same until Norman Berkowitz had passed.

Norman was Sonya's boyfriend. In the evenings he called her up and they had long conversations about nothing. On Saturdays they sometimes met at McDonald's, as if by accident, and sat around eating French fries for an hour, talking about nothing.

Daphne did the same with Eddie. Meredith did the same with Kirby McEvedy. And Anastasia did the same with Steve.

Since Steve Harvey lived just down the street from Anastasia, he sometimes even stopped by her house after school or on weekends. Steve got a kick out of playing with Sam.

But the rules at school were different. Anastasia hadn't quite figured out *why* they were; but she knew that they were, and so she followed them. It was important, at school, to pretend that you hated the person you actually liked. Just a few minutes before, Steve had passed the girls in the hall; he had grabbed Anastasia's hat off her head and tossed it on top of her locker.

"Harvey, you creep!" Anastasia had yelled. And Steve Harvey had sauntered away.

"That turkey," she had muttered to Sonya as she retrieved her hat. But secretly she was pleased. If Steve had grabbed Sonya's hat, it would have meant everything was over between Steve and Anastasia. Only Norman Berkowitz could grab Sonya's hat.

She and Sonya headed home together through the snowy streets.

"Call me tonight, okay?" said Sonya.

"Okay. I promised I'd call Daphne first, though."

"And I'll see you at McDonald's tomorrow, right? But don't let me eat anything at McDonald's. I'm on a diet."

"Again?" Anastasia grinned. Sonya was always on a diet.

"Right. This time I'm going to stick with it, too, even though tonight'll be tough. My mother always makes a giant dinner on Friday night. I made her promise to give me only a little bit of skinless chicken, though. A microscopic piece. And no dessert."

"You want me to call you right at dinnertime and remind you not to eat?"

Sonya thought about it. "No. But restrain me at McDonald's. Arrrggghh!" she screeched suddenly. A form had darted past the girls; he had smashed a handful of snow against Sonya's bare neck.

"You just watch it, Norman!" she yelled after the fleeing figure. "That Norman Berkowitz," Sonya muttered to Anastasia. "He's *so* asinine." She was flushed with pleasure.

Anastasia glanced around the quiet street, but Steve was nowhere in sight. It was disappointing. She had hoped to get a handful of snow down her neck, too, so that she could scream the way Sonya had.

"Tonight's going to be terrific at my house," she confided in Sonya. "My mother's on a new, organized schedule. I won't be surprised if when I get home, there's a whole batch of oatmeal cookies or something."

"Oatmeal cookies? *Your* mother?"

"Really," said Anastasia. "My father and I fixed it so that my mother's whole life is going to be different. She has no idea that keeping house can be so simple."

>< >< ><

No oatmeal cookies. Anastasia could tell when she entered the kitchen that there were no oatmeal cookies, though she noticed with satisfaction a package of defrosted pork chops sitting on the counter. Well, she thought, Mom's still adjusting; *soon* there will be oatmeal cookies.

"I'm home!" she called, after she dropped her schoolbooks on the table and drank a glass of apple juice.

"Hi!" her mother called back from upstairs.

Anastasia found her mother sitting on Sam's bedroom floor. She and Sam had constructed a large garage from blocks and were lining up Matchbox cars at the entrance.

"They all need inspection stickers," Sam explained, and he drove a little red car into the garage.

"Oh no," Mrs. Krupnik said in a gruff garage mechanic's voice, "bad brakes on this one."

"Bad headlights, too," announced Sam. "This one flunks. Let's junk it."

He drove the red car out of the garage and dropped it into a metal wastebasket with a resounding clunk.

"That's the junkyard," Sam said.

"How was your day, Anastasia?" her mother asked, standing up. "Any more problems with Steve?"

"Actually, it was a pretty good day as far as Steve was concerned. At lunchtime he bumped into the table where I was sitting so that my milk container tipped over. And at the end of school, he grabbed my hat and threw it on top of my locker."

Mrs. Krupnik grinned. "Great," she said.

"*Rrrrrrr,*" Sam said, driving a green car out of the garage. He dropped it into the wastebasket junkyard. "No windshield wipers," he explained happily.

Anastasia sat down on Sam's bed. "You know, Mom," she said, "you really amaze me sometimes. I don't think most mothers would understand about that stuff. Most mothers would probably think it was a *bad* thing, that a boy tipped over your milk and grabbed your hat. I bet Sonya Isaacson's mother would call the boy's mother to complain."

Mrs. Krupnik sat down on the bed beside Anastasia. She smoothed the legs of her paint-spattered jeans. "Well," she said, "for some reason I remember what that was like. When I was in seventh grade — no, maybe it was eighth — I liked a boy named Freddy Valente. Freddy Valente was really neat; he had the longest eyelashes I've ever seen. Except maybe for Sam's."

Sam looked up, grinned, and fluttered his long eyelashes.

"Did he grab your hat?" Anastasia asked.

Mrs. Krupnik blushed. "No, actually, what Freddy Valente was into was bra snapping. He used to come up behind me in the hall and snap my bra."

Anastasia giggled.

"So of course I would shriek and scream and pretend to be outraged."

Anastasia nodded. "Of course," she said.

Sam had stopped junking cars and was listening with interest. "How do you snap a bra?" he asked.

Mrs. Krupnik knelt on the floor with her back toward Sam. "Just pull it," she said, "and then let it snap back."

Sam frowned, with his tongue between his teeth. Carefully he snapped his mother's bra.

"Ouch," Mrs. Krupnik said.

Sam giggled, and snapped it again.

His mother stood up. "Enough," she said. "Somehow the thrill is gone. It was much more exciting when Freddy Valente did it."

"I wonder what ever happened to him," Anastasia said. She pictured Freddy Valente grown up, a long-eyelashed bra snapper, maybe looking like Burt Reynolds. Someone like that might have quite a glamorous career.

"He's a dentist in Albany," her mother said. "Sorry about that."

Outside, in the driveway, they heard the familiar sound of the Krupnik car arriving. It backfired three times between the street and the garage. Then it sputtered, coughed, and finally gave a long, noisy whine before it was quiet. Anastasia, Sam, and their mother all went to the window and looked down. In a moment they saw Dr. Krupnik emerge from the garage with his briefcase in one hand and a pile of papers in the other. His pipe was clenched between his teeth. At the rear of the car he turned and kicked the back bumper angrily. Then he headed toward the house.

"He really hates that car," murmured Mrs. Krupnik. "I wish we could afford a new one."

"Then we could junk this one," said Sam. *"Rrrrrrr."*

"I bet anything he swore at it," Anastasia commented. "I hope the neighbors didn't hear him."

They all went downstairs. As usual, Dr. Krupnik was quite cheerful when he came through the back door. As soon as he was away from the car, his good disposition always returned.

"Greetings," he said. He set his briefcase down, picked up Sam, and gave him a hug. "Hey, Sam, what on earth are you doing?" he asked. Sam had reached inside his father's coat.

"I'm sneaking my arm around to your back," Sam explained, "because I'm going to snap your bra."

Dr. Krupnik put Sam back down on the floor. "You're going to find that the world is full of disappointments, sport," he said. "Hey! Look at that! Do you see that, Anastasia?"

He was pointing to the package of pork chops. Anastasia looked, and nodded.

"I knew it," said her father as he hung up his coat. "Katherine, I knew it would work. We're going to have a great gourmet pork chop dinner, all because of that fabulous schedule, right?"

"Actually," said Mrs. Krupnik, "*wrong.* We are

going to have pork chops for dinner, true. But the schedule, to put it bluntly, stinks." She took a Pyrex dish from the cupboard and began to unwrap the pork chops. "Would you wash some potatoes, Anastasia?" she asked.

Anastasia went to the pantry and took four baking potatoes out of the bag. She took them to the sink. "Why?" she asked. "Why does it stink?"

"It was going like clockwork this morning," said her father. "We all got up at seven, right?"

"Right," said Mrs. Krupnik as she sprinkled the pork chops with thyme.

"I made our bed for a change, right?"

"Right. Thank you."

"Anastasia," said Dr. Krupnik, "did you make your bed?"

Anastasia nodded. She poked the washed potatoes with a knife and put them into a pan. "I made it lumpy," she confessed, "but I did make it."

"And Sam got dressed okay, even though his socks don't match."

Sam looked at his feet. He was wearing one blue sock and one red one. "I wanted them that way," he explained.

"And we all ate breakfast, and then Sam went off with his carpool, and Anastasia left for school, and I left for work, just the way the schedule said we should," Dr. Krupnik went on. "And obviously you remembered to take the pork chops out of the freezer. Let me take another look at the schedule."

Anastasia took the paper from the kitchen bulletin board and handed it to him. She put the potatoes into the oven beside the pork chops.

"Everything went absolutely perfectly up until eight o'clock," said Dr. Krupnik after he had examined the schedule.

"Correct," Mrs. Krupnik said. She sat down at the kitchen table. "Now. Let's talk about *after* eight o'clock, when things began to fall apart."

"Sam," said Dr. Krupnik, "would you go to the refrigerator and get me a beer?"

Forty-five minutes later, Anastasia's father had made a lot of notes on the schedule. "I'll have to rewrite this, it's such a mess," he said.

"The whole day was a mess," said Mrs. Krupnik.

"Well, the pork chops smell good," Anastasia pointed out. "Want me to make a salad?"

Her mother nodded. "Thanks," she said. "Be sure to use up that cucumber. It's really ancient, almost museum quality."

"The problem is," announced Anastasia's father, "that there were a lot of unexpected events. Things we didn't anticipate when we made the schedule."

"There always are," said Mrs. Krupnik. "Every day there are unexpected events."

"That's true, Dad," Anastasia said, looking up from the chopping board where she was slicing the cucumber. "Even in school that's true. Marlene Braverman fainted in Chorus today. Whammo; right out cold on the floor when they were practicing 'Trees.' They got to the part about 'a nest of robins in her hair' and Marlene just keeled over. They took her to the nurse's office, and the nurse said it was because she hadn't eaten breakfast or lunch."

"Maybe Marlene Braverman's mother doesn't have a housekeeping schedule," suggested Mrs. Krupnik, "and so she forgot to make breakfast."

"I had an unexpected event in nursery school, too," Sam said. "I spilled my juice all over the table. It turned the cookies into moosh."

"Well," Dr. Krupnik said, making some final

notes on the housekeeping schedule, "Anastasia and I should have thought of that. But now I've redone the list, with special allowances for unexpected events. Things should run absolutely smoothly now, Katherine."

She sighed.

"I'll recopy this after dinner," he said, and went to tack it to the bulletin board again. He picked up the stack of papers he'd been carrying when he came into the house. "Here's the mail, by the way. You forgot to get the mail out of the mailbox today." He glanced through the envelopes, tossed a couple of them unopened into the wastebasket, and handed Mrs. Krupnik some others.

"Look at this gorgeous salad," Anastasia announced. She displayed the wooden bowl. "I bet nobody in the whole world except me would have thought of putting sliced banana into a salad. I bet I'm going to be a really creative cook someday."

"What're those little brown things?" asked her father, peering into the salad.

"Peanuts!"

"Peanuts and bananas in a salad?" he asked, frowning.

"It'll be great," said Anastasia happily. "Don't you think it'll be great, Mom?"

"What?" Her mother looked up from the letter she was reading. "Sure." She looked back down at the letter.

"Maybe I should think about becoming a chef for a career," said Anastasia. "None of my other choices worked out very well. Ballet dancing, or being an author. But I think I have a real flair for cooking, don't you, Mom?"

Her mother glanced up again with a distracted look. "A real flair for cooking," she said. "How do you feel about creative housekeeping in general?"

Anastasia shrugged.

"Think you could manage this household if you had a carefully thought-out nonsexist housekeeping schedule?" her mother asked.

"Of course," Anastasia said. "Organized housekeeping is ridiculously easy, once you have a schedule."

Her mother gave her an odd smile.

"Why?" asked Anastasia suspiciously.

But the telephone rang before her mother could answer. Dr. Krupnik picked it up. "Yes," they could hear him say, "she's here, but we're about to eat dinner. Could you call her back a little later?"

He came back from the telephone chuckling. "It was Steve Harvey, Anastasia," he said. "He'll call you back. And he has a new name for you, by the way. I was wrong when I said that he would run out of new names."

"What's this one?" asked Anastasia, cringing.

"He has a real way with words," her father said.

"WHAT'S THIS ONE?"

"Anaconda," Dr. Krupnik said. "He asked if Anaconda Krupnik was home."

"What does it mean?"

"It's very imaginative. I wonder if he's using a dictionary, or if he actually has a highly developed vocabulary."

"DAD! *What does it mean?*"

"It's a South American snake," her father explained. "A kind of python."

"You're in charge, Anastasia," her mother said, looking up again from the letter that she seemed to be reading for the tenth time.

"How can I be in charge when I can't figure out how to get even? What if he calls me that in *school?*

What if the other kids know that it's a python? How can I defend myself, for Pete's sake?" Anastasia wailed.

Her mother was smiling. "I meant that you are in charge of the house," she said. "Starting Monday."

They all looked at her. Even Sam, who had flung himself to the floor and was starting to do a python imitation under the kitchen table, slithered back out and looked up curiously.

"What do you mean?" Anastasia asked finally.

"I'm flying to Los Angeles, Monday," Mrs. Krupnik said. "A book that I illustrated is being made into an animated film. They want me to act as adviser."

"Monday?" asked Dr. Krupnik. "That's just two days away. They can't give you such short notice."

Mrs. Krupnik handed him the letter. "They apologize for the short notice," she said. "Take a look at what they're going to pay me."

He looked and blinked. "Holy moley," he said.

"How long will you be gone?" Anastasia asked.

"Ten days."

Ten days!" said Anastasia. "I can't—how do you expect me to—"

Mrs. Krupnik stood up and took the silverware

from a drawer. "I'll set the table tonight," she said, "since you made the salad."

"How on earth can a thirteen-year-old person—"

"Easy," her mother said. "You have this wonderful schedule."

Krupnik Family Nonsexist Housekeeping Schedule

Version 2

7:00 A.M.   Everyone gets up.
             Anastasia makes bed.
             Myron makes bed.
             Katherine makes Sam's bed.
             Katherine helps Sam dress.
             Katherine makes breakfast.
             Everyone eats.

8:00 A.M.   Katherine takes food out of freezer.
             Myron and Anastasia leave for work and
             school.
             Nursery school carpool picks up Sam.
             Katherine goes to work in the studio.

INSERT: Unexpected event. For example, furnace makes
odd sound like small explosion. Katherine calls gas
company. Repairman comes and tracks muddy snow onto
kitchen floor. K. has to clean kitchen floor.
Unexpected event #2. Anastasia calls from school to say
that she has forgotten to feed Frank, her goldfish, and
would like Katherine to do it. Katherine argues that Frank
will survive a few more hours without food but Anastasia
expresses grave concern over Frank's welfare and
her future affection for her mother should Frank die of
starvation. Katherine goes to third floor to feed Frank.

10:00 A.M.   Katherine's coffee break. (Has to be eliminated
             if there are unexpected events. See above.)

NOON   Carpool brings Sam home.

INSERT: Unexpected event. Sam's carpool driver has flat
tire and arrives forty-five minutes late. In meantime
Katherine has called nursery school in panic. Nursery
school calls police, police finally locate car and
assist carpool driver. Katherine sits frantically by
phone wondering if Sam has been kidnaped.

Katherine and Sam have lunch. (This is postponed until
later in case of unexpected events. See above.)

1:00 P.M.   Clothes into washing machine.
             Sam and Katherine do shopping.

INSERT: Unexpected event. Katherine discovers, walking
home from grocery store, that Sam has shoplifted package
of Dentyne gum. Return to store so that store owner can
have serious moralistic talk with Sam.

2:00 P.M.   Clothes into dryer. (Postponed if unexpected
             events. See above.)
             Sam takes nap. (Preceded by long talk about
             shoplifting. See above.)
             Katherine works in studio. (Canceled in
             case of unexpected events. See above.)

3:00 P.M.   Sam and Katherine fold clean laundry.

INSERT: Unexpected event. Discovery, upon removing wash,
that Myron's black socks have been included with white
things, requiring white things to be rewashed with
bleach to remove dye.

             They play. (Postponed in case of unexpected
             events. See above.)

4:00 P.M.   Katherine starts dinner.
             Anastasia comes home from school.

5:00 P.M.   Myron gets home.

6:00 P.M.   Anastasia sets table.
             Everyone eats.

(All of the above is adjusted according to unexpected events.)

7:00 P.M.   Katherine, Myron, or Anastasia does dishes,
             depending on whose turn.

8:00 P.M.   Someone bathes Sam and puts him to bed.

*** vacuuming, window-washing, etc., on Saturdays

three

$\mathcal{A}$nastasia sat on her parents' bed on Sunday evening, watching her mother pack. From the nearby bathroom came the sounds of her father bathing Sam.

"I'm worried about several things, Mom," Anastasia said.

Her mother looked up from folding a silk blouse. "Really?" she asked. "Like what?"

Anastasia arranged her legs underneath herself so that she was sitting like Buddha. "Well," she said, "don't be insulted or anything, but I'm afraid you're not going to go over real well on this trip."

Mrs. Krupnik placed the blouse in the suitcase and began taking some dresses out of her closet. "I'm not?

Why not? I did terrific illustrations for that book. It was that really sophisticated children's book, remember—the one about the wedding of two gazelles? It won some awards."

"No, it's not your work, Mom," Anastasia explained. "You're one of the best illustrators around. It's a couple of other things. One is your clothes."

"My *clothes?*" Mrs. Krupnik held up the blue silk dress she was about to pack. "What's wrong with my clothes? I should have had this cleaned, I suppose, but there wasn't time. And it's not *grossly* dirty, just sort of vaguely smelling of perfume from the last time I wore it." She sniffed the dress. "It really is perfume, Anastasia, not perspiration or anything."

"Mom, it's not the condition of your clothes. It's the *style.*"

"What's wrong with the style?" Her mother looked at the simple blue dress again, puzzled.

"Mom, when you're on the Coast—and incidentally, you're supposed to call it the Coast, not California or Los Angeles—"

"I am? How do you know that?"

"From magazines."

"Oh. Well, I'll practice on the plane. I'll practice saying, 'Hello. It's so nice to be here on the Coast.'"

"Make sure it sounds casual. It has to sound casual."

"I'll try. What's wrong with this dress?"

"Mom, on the Coast, you're supposed to *glitter.*"

"I'm supposed to *what?*"

"Glitter. You're supposed to be, well, *glitzy.*"

Her mother frowned at her. "Anastasia, I don't know what you're talking about. All of a sudden you're speaking a foreign language. Can you give me an example of glitzy?"

Anastasia chewed on a strand of hair. "Well, do you by any chance have any leather pants?"

"Good grief. Of course I don't have any leather pants. You know that. You're always prowling around in my closet, trying to find something to borrow."

"Well, it's an example. You asked for an example. If you had leather pants, you could wear those, and then you could put that dress *over* the leather pants, like a giant blouse, and around the waist you could put a big cowboy belt. And huge earrings, of course."

Her mother was making a terrible face. "Then I'd glitter?" she asked.

"Yeah, I think so."

Mrs. Krupnik sighed and put the blue dress into the suitcase. "I've decided I don't want to glitter. Huge earrings make my ears hurt. It wouldn't be any fun to glitter if I had an earache. I guess I'll just be the only unglittery person in Los Angeles—excuse me, I mean on the Coast. Maybe that will make me seem interesting."

Anastasia was dubious. She thought it would make her mother seem boring. "There's another thing, too," she said. "The way you talk."

Her mother took a pair of shoes out of the closet, licked her finger, and rubbed a smudged spot off one. "Do they talk differently out there?" she asked.

Anastasia nodded. "I know you can't learn it all in one evening," she said. "But I could just teach you a few expressions, and then you could fake it."

"Okay. Teach me one."

"Well, if something happens that you don't like—say, for example, they tell you that they want you to redo the gazelles—"

"They won't. Those gazelles are perfect."

"It's just an example, Mom. If they tell you that, you should say, 'Make my day.'"

"'Make my day'?" Her mother made the same sort of face she had made about the glittering. "I don't understand what that means, even."

Anastasia stood up. "Here, I'll show you. It's all in the inflection. It has to be casual, and bored, and sarcastic. You play the part of the film producer, okay? And I'll be you. Tell me I have to redo the gazelles."

Her mother grinned and put down the shoes. She glanced around, picked up a ballpoint pen from the dresser, and clamped it between her teeth like a cigar. "Here's the thing, Ms. Krupnik," she said in a deep, harsh voice. "We're going to need a whole new set of gazelles here, something a little cuter, you get the idea?" She flicked some ashes from the imaginary cigar.

Anastasia leaned in a casual, languid pose against the bedpost. She looked at her mother, the film producer, with a bored stare, her eyes half closed. In a low, sarcastic voice, she said, "Like, maaake my *daaay.*"

Her mother dropped the ballpoint cigar and

roared with laughter. "I love it," she said. "I *love* it, Anastasia."

She picked the shoes back up and put them into the suitcase. "But I can't do it. It just isn't me."

Anastasia flopped back down on the bed. She handed her mother some pantyhose that were waiting to be packed. She sighed. "Well," she said, "I just sincerely hope that you're not too humiliated out there."

Sam dashed into the room, naked and giggling. He glanced over his shoulder and called, "You can't catch me!" He dropped to the floor and disappeared under his parents' bed.

Dr. Krupnik appeared at the door with Sam's pajamas in his hand. "Where did he go?" he asked.

Anastasia and her mother pointed under the bed. "He's going to need another whole bath, Myron," Mrs. Krupnik said. "There are a thousand dust balls under there. I forgot to vacuum yesterday, even though it was on the schedule."

Sam's carpool driver honked in the driveway in the morning. Sam kissed his mother goodbye, pulled on his mittens, and trudged out through the snow to the car. Before he got in, he turned and waved cheerfully toward the kitchen window.

"I've never been away from Sam before," said Mrs. Krupnik after she had waved back and the car had driven away. "What a strange feeling."

"We'll take good care of him, Mom," Anastasia said.

She sighed. "I know you will. It's all set with the nursery school. They'll keep him for lunch and for the afternoon session. He'll be home by three-thirty every day. Now you be sure to be here, Anastasia. They won't leave him at an empty house."

"I will, Mom, I promise. It's going to ruin my social life for ten days. But I'll be home by three thirty."

A backfire sounded from the garage. Then another. Anastasia and her mother looked out the window and saw clouds of black smoke coming from the tailpipe of the car.

"He'll have the car warmed up in a minute," Anastasia said. "Did he take your suitcase?"

"It's in the trunk of the car." Mrs. Krupnik put on her coat. "Now, let's see — am I forgetting anything?"

"Tickets?"

"I'm picking them up at the airport."

Anastasia looked around the kitchen. "We all forgot the breakfast dishes," she pointed out. "But I'll do them when I get home from school."

"Right." Her mother pulled on her gloves, picked up her briefcase, and headed for the door. "You're in charge, Anastasia. I'll call you tomorrow night, just to make sure everything's okay."

"It will be, Mom. I'm a very organized person, you know."

"All right, then. I'm off." Her mother gave her a hug. Anastasia watched through the window as she got into the car, which jerked and bounced down the driveway toward the street. She kept waving until it was out of sight.

Then Anastasia got into her ski jacket and hat. She collected her schoolbooks and was halfway down the back steps before she remembered something and turned back.

"I almost blew it the first day," she said to herself. Quickly she went to the freezer, pulled out a package of rock-hard hamburger, and deposited it on the drain board of the kitchen sink.

"Okay," she said, glancing at the schedule tacked

to the bulletin board. "None of the beds is made, but I'll do that when I get home. Meat's out of the freezer. Breakfast dishes can wait. And if I don't leave this instant, I'm going to be late for school."

She headed for the door again. The telephone rang.

She hesitated.

It rang again. She went back and answered it.

"Ms. Krupnik?" asked a bubbly voice.

"Yeah."

"E-Z Telephone Shopping!" the voice said. "Anybody in your family in need of new underwear? We're having a special!"

Anastasia blinked. "That's a very personal question," she said.

"How about blankets?" the voice asked.

Anastasia looked at her watch. She was definitely going to be late for school. Talk about Unexpected Events. "The blanket on my brother's bed is kind of ratty," she said. "It was his security blanket when he was younger, so he used to suck on it, and chew on it, all the time, and now he doesn't do that, but the blanket is all messed up."

"How many new ones would you like?" the voice asked. "And what color?"

"Blue, I guess. Just one."

"Twin, full, queen, or king?"

Anastasia thought. "Twin," she said.

"Standard, or electric?"

"Stand — no, wait. Electric. Sam would like electric. He likes to fool with switches."

"Sheets or towels?"

Anastasia groaned. She didn't have time to think about sheets or towels. "No," she said. "Thank you," she added.

"Credit card number?"

Oh, *no.* "Just a minute," Anastasia said. "I have to get it."

She dashed to her father's study and opened the second drawer of his desk. There, in a typed list, were all of their credit card numbers. She ran back to the phone and read the MasterCard number to the voice.

"I really have to go," she said. "I'm late."

"Bye, now," said the voice.

Anastasia picked up her books again and headed

off for school. Already it wasn't quite as easy as she had anticipated, being in charge.

She arrived home just a few minutes before Sam. Anastasia was mad. All of her friends had stayed after school for a basketball game. The streets were absolutely deserted as she walked home, and she imagined that she could hear the cheering junior high crowd back there at the gym. She imagined that Steve Harvey was making basket after basket and was wondering why she hadn't stayed to cheer for him.

Back home, there were three unmade beds — she had pulled the covers up hastily — and a sink full of dishes with congealed egg on them.

And Sam was bratty. He was tired after an unaccustomed day at school, and he whined. He wanted Anastasia to play trucks with him.

"I can't play trucks," Anastasia said. "I have to do these dishes."

"Mom always plays trucks," Sam whimpered.

Anastasia looked at him in exasperation. "Tell you what," she suggested finally. "Bring your trucks down here and you can transport the clean dishes to the cupboard."

He trotted off and returned with a large red dump truck. On his hands and knees he *rrrrrrrr*ed each clean dish to the pantry and put it away. Anastasia waited impatiently, holding cups and glasses after they were dry, for the trucking company to return for a pickup.

When the last one was done, she hung up the dishtowel and wiped the sink with a sponge. She sat down wearily in a kitchen chair, and Sam climbed into her lap.

"Scratch my back," he said. "My back itches."

Automatically Anastasia scratched his little back through his shirt.

"More," Sam said when she stopped.

Anastasia sighed and scratched again. She was still scratching when the back door opened and her father appeared.

"Greetings," he said. "Your mom's in sunny California by now!"

"You're home early," Anastasia began, but then she looked at her watch. "How did it get to be five o'clock?" she asked.

Sam flopped himself around in her lap. "Scratch my front," he said. "My front itches, too."

Anastasia lifted him down to the floor. "I can't," she told him. "I have to start dinner. What vegetable do you guys want? Corn okay?"

"Sure," said her father. "Good thing I remembered to take some meat out of the freezer."

"Yeah," said Anastasia. "I was halfway down the back steps before I remembered to—what do you mean, *you* remembered?"

Her father went to the pantry and came back with a plate full of something, which he set on the table.

"Chicken breasts," he announced. "I remembered just before I went out to warm up the car this morning."

Anastasia looked at the chicken breasts in dismay. She took her own package of meat from the side of the sink. "But I thawed out hamburger!" she wailed.

Sam looked at both of them. Then he trotted off to the small counter beside the refrigerator, the one where the toaster stood. He reached up, pushed aside the toaster, and took down a package.

"Hot dogs," he announced. "I did hot dogs."

Anastasia stared at the hamburger. Then she

stared at the chicken breasts. Then she stared at the hot dogs.

"Well," she said flatly, "make my day."

"Actually," her father replied, "I think what we have to make is a new schedule."

Sam sat down on the kitchen floor and began to cry. "Make me stop itching!" he howled. "I itch *all over!*"

Krupnik Family Nonsexist Housekeeping Schedule

Version 3

7:00 A.M. Everyone gets up.
           Nobody bothers making beds. They only get
           slept in again anyway.
           Anastasia feeds Frank Goldfish.
           Myron helps Sam get dressed.

7:30 A.M. Everybody eats cold cereal.
           Anastasia rinses dishes. Detergent is not
           required for cold cereal dishes.
           ANASTASIA takes something out of the freezer
           for dinner.

8:00 A.M. Everybody leaves.
           Do not go back to answer phone. Only go
           back if house is on fire, or something.

3:30 P.M. Anastasia and Sam come home.
           They do laundry.

5:00 P.M. Myron comes home.
           Anastasia and Myron cook dinner.
           Everybody eats, from paper plates.
           Throw away paper plates.

EVENING: Someone puts Sam to bed. Sam does not need
           a bath every night, only if he is unusually
           grubby.
           Anastasia does homework.
If Katherine calls, NOBODY TELLS KATHERINE
ABOUT CHANGE IN HOUSEKEEPING RULES.

Saturday: vacuuming, window-washing, etc.

four

𝒜nastasia opened her eyes sleepily when her father called "Seven o'clock!" up the stairs to her third-floor bedroom. She groaned. Why was it so hard to get up in the morning?

Frank, her goldfish, was swimming in circles, chasing his own tail around his bowl. Frank was always wide awake and cheerful in the mornings. He was the kind of guy who would go jogging at dawn, if he had legs.

Groggily, she reached over to the fish food box and tapped some into Frank's bowl. If only she could do *all* the household chores without getting out of bed.

"You and I have very little in common, Frank,"

Anastasia said, yawning, "except that we both like to eat."

Frank stared out at her with his bulging eyes through the side of the bowl. He flipped his tail.

Down on the second floor, she could hear sounds: the shower running, her father's feet squeaking in the bathtub, and Sam—Anastasia groaned and got out of bed. Sam was crying again. Ordinarily Sam *never* cried; once she had seen him fall right over the railing of the back porch, head over heels, into a prickly bush. Then he had climbed out of the bush, covered with scratches, brushed himself off, remarked, "Ouch," and gone scampering off to find his tricycle.

But last night he had cried and cried. He hadn't eaten any dinner—even though there were several choices—and he had complained about a hundred different things. His head hurt. His toes itched. His nose ached. His belly button felt too tight.

Finally he had fallen asleep on the hard linoleum floor of the kitchen while Anastasia and her father ate.

"What a hypochondriac," Anastasia had said, whispering, so that he wouldn't wake up and start wailing again.

"He just misses his mom," Dr. Krupnik had pointed out.

They had both looked at Sam curled into a sleeping ball on the floor. "Should we wake him up for his bath?" Dr. Krupnik had asked.

Anastasia had shaken her head. "He's not that dirty. And if we wake him up he'll just start missing Mom again, and crying. Let's just put him to bed with his clothes on."

Dr. Krupnik had frowned. "He'll wet the bed if we don't take him to the bathroom."

It was true. They had both thought about that. "Well," said Anastasia finally, "I think I'd rather change his sheets tomorrow than listen to him howl anymore tonight."

Her father had nodded. "Me too," he agreed. Carefully, he had scooped Sam up and carried him upstairs to his bed. "By morning, after a good night's sleep," he had said when he came back down, "he'll be fine. It's just a difficult adjustment."

But now it was morning, and Sam was howling again. Anastasia sighed and pulled on her clothes, noticing as she did that this was the last of her clean underwear. The jeans didn't matter—she had worn these for three days anyway—but she would have to wash underwear after school today. And socks.

She found Sam standing in the hall, his hair damp and matted, his face bright pink, his yesterday's clothes wrinkled and wet.

"I want my pajamas!" Sam yowled.

Anastasia took his hand and led him to his bedroom. "It's morning, Sam. Time to put on clean clothes for school. You can't wear pajamas to school, silly."

"I don't want to go to school," Sam whined as she began taking off his clothes. "I hate school."

Never get sucked into an argument with a three-year-old, Anastasia remembered her mother saying. Because you can't win one. An adult will lose against a three-year-old every time.

"I know," she said soothingly. "Sometimes I hate school, too. But we have to go anyway. There's a *law* that says you have to go to school." She pulled his shirt off over his head. "Now stop crying, because it makes you all sweaty."

Then she stared at him. "Sam," she said, "what are all these spots?"

Sam looked down at his own bare chest dotted with pink. It was so interesting that he stopped crying. "I've turned into a polka-dot person," he said. "Look at me, poking the dots." He began to poke each one with his finger.

Anastasia turned him around. His back, too, was covered with spots.

"Dad?" she called through the closed bathroom door. "Something's wrong with Sam. Something *bit* him! Could we have bedbugs?"

Sam grinned. "Bedbugs," he said. "Millions of bedbugs."

Dr. Krupnik came out of the bathroom, tying his tie. "Of course we don't have bedbugs," he said. Then he looked at Sam. "Holy—"

"Holy moley." Anastasia completed it for him. She finished undressing Sam. "*Look.* Every inch of him."

Now that he was the center of attention, Sam was completely happy. "Every single inch," he announced proudly. Naked, he began to dance around his bedroom. "Puff, the magic bedbug," he sang, "lived by the sea—"

"What's his doctor's name?" Anastasia's father asked. "Didn't your mom leave a list with all the important phone numbers on it? Where is it? I'd better call the doctor."

"He's my doctor, too, Dad," Anastasia said. "Dr. Nazarosian. I'll call him. He's in his office early. The list's right by the phone in your bedroom."

Sam was still prancing around.

"Do you feel okay, Sam?" Anastasia asked. "I need to tell the doctor all your symptoms."

"Tell him I'm like a leopard," Sam suggested. "A spotted leopard." He began to crawl across the rug, growling. "Lookit me, being a leopard," he said. He grabbed the corner of the rug between his teeth and shook it back and forth with a ferocious growl.

"Dr. Nazarosian," Anastasia said on the phone, "this is Anastasia Krupnik. I'm calling because—"

"Anastasia!" he said heartily, interrupting her. "How *are* you? I haven't seen you in ages. You're one of my favorite patients because you're never sick. Don't tell me you're sick!"

"No, I'm not. But my mother is in California, so—"

"California! Getting a little sunshine, is she? Can't say I blame her. I'm getting pretty sick of this snow.

Of course if I had time to take a vacation and do a little skiing, I might feel differently. Do you ski?"

"No," said Anastasia, looking at her watch. She was going to be late for school *again*. "I'm calling because I'm in charge, and it's about Sam. Sam's—"

He interrupted her again. "Good old Sam—my very favorite patient, with all due respect, Anastasia. Remember the time Sam fell out the window and—"

This time Anastasia interrupted *him*. "Dr. Nazarosian," she said, "Sam's entire body is covered with pink spots."

He chuckled. "Not surprising," he said. "Not at all surprising."

Anastasia was taken aback. Not surprising to be covered with pink spots? *She* found it surprising. What on earth *would* surprise Dr. Nazarosian? Blue spots, maybe? Green?

"They're even on his ears," she went on.

"How old is Sam now—three?" the doctor asked. "Let me get his chart out. Here it is. Three years old, like I thought. Does he go to nursery school?"

"Yes," said Anastasia. She told him the name of Sam's school.

"I should have guessed. Half the kids in that nursery school have it. The other half will by next week. Except for a few. There are always a few who for some reason seem to be immune. We've never been able to figure that out. And then sometimes the ones who don't get it when they're three suddenly come down with it as *adults,* for some reason, even though they were undoubtedly exposed to it when they were young—"

"Exposed to *what?*"

"Chicken pox," the doctor said. "Sam has chicken pox."

Anastasia's father came into the room and looked at her quizzically. He pointed to his watch at the same time.

"I don't need to see him, unless he has special problems," the doctor was going on. "Give him a little Children's Tylenol for the fever. And if he itches—well, that was a foolish thing to say; of *course* he itches—add some baking soda to a bath and let him soak in that. He'll feel fine in a day or two. But of course he'll have to stay out of school until the lesions heal. Well, that was a foolish thing to say, too; they're probably going to close that school down for a couple of weeks. Can't run a school when everybody has chicken pox, now, can you?" He chuckled.

Anastasia looked up at her father and mouthed the words "chicken pox."

"Chicken pox?" her father mouthed back.

"Now, let me just get out *your* chart and see if you've had chicken pox, Anastasia," the doctor was saying.

"I had it when I was—"

"Here we are. Krupnik, Anastasia. You were right in the filing cabinet next to your brother. Let's see, you're thirteen now. Pretty soon you won't even need a pediatrician. For heaven's sake, look at this—"

"I had chicken pox when I was—"

"I'd forgotten all about that time we had to pump your stomach when you were two. You ate ant poison. Well, that's nothing compared to what *some* toddlers eat. I had one who drank a whole bottle of Windex once. Wouldn't you think it would taste terrible? Now, let's see, you had an ear infection that same year, and—"

"I had chicken pox when I was four years old."

"Here we are. You had chicken pox when you were four years old, Anastasia."

Anastasia sighed.

"Well, kiddo," Dr. Nazarosian went on, "I'd love to chat with you a bit longer, but you know how it is. Duty calls. Half the mothers in this town are trying to get me on the phone right at this very minute, and you know why?"

"Because their kids have—"

"Because their kids have chicken pox, that's why. Now, you call again if Sam has any complications. But he should be just fine, maybe a little irritable until the fever goes down, that's all."

Anastasia heard a sound and glanced over. Sam had wandered into the room, still naked, holding a Magic Marker. He was carefully drawing green lines from one pink spot to the next across his chest. He looked up and grinned. "Follow the dots," he said.

Anastasia said goodbye politely to the doctor and hung up.

Sam handed her his underpants and socks. "Help me get dressed for school," he said.

Anastasia sighed. "We can't go to school," she told him. "You can't go to school because you have chicken pox, and I can't go to school, unless—" She looked hopefully at her father.

But he shook his head. "I'm sorry, Anastasia," he said, "but I have a lecture scheduled at nine o'clock, and a department meeting after that, and I'm giving an exam at one, and—well, I'll try to get home early. I'm sorry."

Sam's face puckered and he began to cry again. "There's a *law* that you have to go to school!" he wailed. "I *want* to go to school! I want to show everybody my dots!"

"Well, you *can't*," Anastasia said irritably. She wandered into his room and picked up his clothes from the floor. She began to pull the wet sheets off his bed.

"I guess I'll do laundry this morning," she muttered. "And good grief, we haven't even had breakfast yet."

The telephone rang.

"Good morning," said a spirited voice. "This is the National Telephone Survey Association. Do you have a few minutes to spare to participate in an important poll?"

Anastasia sat down with the laundry in her lap

and balanced the phone on her shoulder. "I guess so," she answered grudgingly. At least it would be more interesting than laundry.

Then she gave her opinion on various political issues for fifteen minutes while Sam sat at her feet and connected the dots on his legs with green ink.

By four in the afternoon Anastasia was rewriting the entire housekeeping schedule. She was exhausted. And she was mad.

She had done all the laundry, and after she had done the laundry, she had decided to vacuum, even though it wasn't Saturday. And when she ran the vacuum cleaner under her parents' bed, it had made a strangling noise and died.

"It ate something it wasn't supposed to," Sam said solemnly. She had been trying to keep Sam in bed — she had even dressed him in his pajamas — but he kept getting out.

So she took the vacuum cleaner apart, unwound a wire coat hanger, and poked it through the vacuum cleaner hose, and out came three of Dr. Krupnik's socks. She peered under the bed, and there were at least six others that the vacuum cleaner hadn't eaten.

Then she found her father's pajamas behind a chair, on the floor.

So she had a whole new stack of laundry and made another trip to the washing machine. No wonder she was exhausted. And no wonder she was mad. She was mad at her father for leaving his dirty clothes all over the place; but mostly she was mad at the telephone. It had been ringing all day. Total strangers had been calling her all day.

Now, at four o'clock, just when she was about to relax with a cup of hot chocolate with a marshmallow in it, the phone rang again.

Angrily she picked it up and began talking before the other person had a chance.

"*No,*" Anastasia said assertively. "I do not want to be part of an important political poll.

"I do not want to have my family's photographs taken even if it is a special offer and includes a gold-painted plastic frame.

"I have absolutely zero interest in a full set of encyclopedias.

"I do not want to test a new gelatin dessert, even if it *is* free of charge.

"I have all the magazine subscriptions that I need, and furthermore"—she took a deep breath—"I am not going to donate money to *anything* even if it *is* a good cause, because I don't *have* any money."

She was about to slam the receiver down when she recognized the voice at the other end.

"Well," said Steve Harvey sarcastically, "I suppose that means you don't want to go to the movies Friday night, either, even though I was willing to pay."

Anastasia gulped. "Hi, Steve," she said in a meek voice.

"Why weren't you in school?"

"My brother is sick, and my mother's away, so I'm in charge, and—" Anastasia talked on, explaining to Steve, but her mind was on what he had said. Had he asked her to go to the movies Friday night? And he would pay? Didn't that make it a *date?*

Anastasia had never had a date in her life. She had *daydreamed* about having a date, and she had even daydreamed about having a date with Steve Harvey. Sure, she had played tennis with Steve in the summer; and sure, she and he had gone to the movies with groups of kids; and once or twice they had even gone just the two of them—but she had always paid her own way, so it didn't count as a date.

Sam was watching her with interest. He had finished his own hot chocolate and was starting on hers. Good thing she'd already had chicken pox, Anastasia thought, because Sam was slurping chicken pox germs right into her cup. Well, that wasn't important. What was important was that Steve Harvey was actually calling and asking her for a date—the first one of her life—and she was worried about what she would wear, how she would act, what they would talk about, whether he would put his arm around her in the movie theater, and . . .

"Anastasia? Are you still there?" Steve asked.

"Yeah."

"Will you be in school tomorrow?"

She sighed. "I won't be there all week. I have to stay with Sam and take care of him and the house. Next week my father's going to do it until my mom gets home next Wednesday, and . . ."

Good grief. She was babbling, and being boring. If she was that boring when they had a date, he would never ask her for another date; he would probably ask someone like Marlene Braverman, and her whole life would be . . .

"Well, can you go to the movies Friday night?" Steve was asking.

"Sure."

"My dad'll drive us and pick us up afterward."

"Okay. Fine." Anastasia tried to sound casual, as if this happened all the time.

"Sam!" she squealed, after she had hung up. "Guess what! I have a date Friday night with Steve Harvey!"

Sam glanced up from the cup of hot chocolate. "Watch this," he said. "It's like the vacuum cleaner, with Daddy's socks." He consumed the melted marshmallow with a loud sucking noise.

Well, thought Anastasia, Sam's too young to understand the significance. Wait till Dad gets home and I tell *him*.

But when her father came through the door at five, he was not his usual cheerful self. His shoulders sagged, and his face had a terrible look. He put his briefcase down, hung up his coat slowly, and sat down on a kitchen chair.

"How's Sam?" he asked, finally, in a disheartened voice.

"Fine," said Anastasia. "Just look at him."

Sam was running a truck around the kitchen floor. His chicken pox spots were all connected by green ink lines, even on his face, which he had done in front of the mirror, and he was making truck noises very happily.

Dr. Krupnik stared gloomily at the floor after glancing at Sam. Wait'll I tell him my news, thought Anastasia with glee. Wait till we tell Mom on the phone tonight. They'll both be so excited. It's the first time one of their children has ever had a real date.

"Did you have a bad day, Dad?" Anastasia asked sympathetically. She was feeling so happy that she decided not even to tell him about *her* bad day, with the endless phone calls from strangers wanting to sell her things. She wasn't even going to bug him about his dirty socks under the bed, or show him the new housekeeping schedule that she had made in a fit of anger.

"I don't want to talk about it," he muttered.

Anastasia tried to remember what her mother would do at times like this. She went to the refrigerator and got her father a can of beer. She took out a box of crackers and some cheese, and put them on the table beside him. She ran to the study, put a record on the stereo, and turned it up loud enough so that they could hear it in the kitchen.

Her father brightened a little, and sipped at the beer. "Vivaldi," he said.

Wait'll I tell him; wait'll I tell him, thought Anastasia, almost shivering with delight.

"Dad," she started, "guess what!"

He stared at her and took another sip of beer. "What?" he asked, finally.

"I have a date Friday night!" Anastasia said with pride, and waited for his reaction.

But to her surprise, he didn't smile. He didn't move. He only stared into the beer can as if he were trying to memorize the ingredients of Miller Lite for a quiz.

Finally he looked up. "So do I," he said in a voice filled with despair.

Krupnik Family Extremely Sexist Housekeeping Schedule

Version 4

7:00 A.M.   Everyone gets up.
             Everyone eats breakfast.

8:00 A.M.   Myron leaves.
             Anastasia stays home and does nothing but
grimy household tasks all day long, and answers the
phone continually, and never even has a chance to read
a book or anything. Sam just watches stupid TV shows
which have no educational value at all or else he follows Anastasia around, whining, and doesn't help with
anything, and whatever she offers him for lunch, he
just says "Blecch" and does barfing imitations.

NIGHT: Everybody goes to bed, wearing clean pajamas
because Anastasia has been standing over a hot washing
machine all day long, but probably no one will even
notice that, much less say "Thank you."

NOTE: When Mom calls, DO NOT MENTION new housekeeping
schedule, or CHICKEN POX or SCHOOL.

*** Vacuuming and window-washing — Forget it.

five

"Dad," Anastasia said, "don't be ridiculous. You can't have a date. You're a married man."

"I know," he said miserably.

"You're a happily married man." She stared at him. "Aren't you? Aren't you happily married?"

"Of course. I'm just about the most happily married man in the whole world. Probably if they had a Mr. and Mrs. Happy Marriage Contest, your mother and I would win."

"Yuck," said Anastasia. She hated the Miss America contest more than any other program on TV. Every year she stayed up late to watch it, just because she hated it so much. The thought of a Mr. and Mrs. Happy Marriage Contest was so disgusting, she could hardly stand it. Still, it was reassuring to know that her parents would win.

"Sam, don't scratch," she said, glancing at Sam, who had stopped driving his truck across the floor in order to scratch a chicken pox spot on his neck.

"Well, I itch," Sam said matter-of-factly.

"After dinner I'll give you a bath in baking powder, like the doctor said." Then Anastasia thought about it. "Or did he say baking soda? Are they the same thing?" she asked her father.

He shrugged. "I suppose so," he said gloomily.

"Dad, cheer up. We have all these good leftovers for dinner: hot dogs, chicken, and hamburger. Quit looking so depressed. Why did you even say that, that you had a date? If you were joking, why aren't you laughing?"

"Anastasia, I wasn't joking. Annie's back. This afternoon I got a phone call at my office, and it was Annie."

"ANNIE!" Anastasia sat down and stared at her father. He *wasn't* joking, then. Even Sam stopped scratching and looked up with interest. Even Sam knew about Annie.

Annie had been Dr. Krupnik's first love. It had

been years and years ago, before he ever met Anastasia's mother. But he had dedicated his first book of poems to Annie—it was still there, on a bookshelf in the study—and when Mrs. Krupnik showed her husband's poetry to people, she never bothered taking that book down.

Annie was an artist. They still had one of her paintings hanging in the living room. Every now and then, Mrs. Krupnik would say, "I wish you'd get rid of that, Myron."

And Dr. Krupnik would glance at the painting and say, "Annie was a fine painter. She was a fine person, too. You'd like her, Katherine."

Katherine Krupnik would make a noise that sounded like "Hmmpph."

Annie had broken Dr. Krupnik's heart, years ago, when she went off to Guatemala to paint. She had wanted him to go with her. But Dr. Krupnik was afraid of snakes, and he read somewhere that there were a lot of snakes in Guatemala. Also, he couldn't speak Spanish, which is what they speak in Guatemala.

So he didn't go, but his heart was broken, he had told Anastasia. His heart was broken for about six months, and then it was mended because he had met another artist, and this one was named Katherine, and he had married her because she was afraid of snakes too, and would never want to go to Guatemala.

And they had lived happily ever after, thought Anastasia, and would even win a disgusting Mr. and Mrs. Happy Marriage Contest if there were one.

But now Annie was back.

"Don't scratch, Sam," Anastasia said again automatically when she saw her brother's hand sneaking up behind his ear.

"Dad," she asked, "how long has it been since you've seen Annie?"

He calculated. "Sixteen years?" he suggested uncertainly. "I'm not sure. A long time, though."

"Why on earth would she call up someone she hadn't seen in sixteen years?" asked Anastasia angrily. "That's stupid. She shouldn't have called you."

He sighed. "No, it's not. She and I were friends."

Anastasia looked at him skeptically. "That's not the way you used to tell it. You were in love with each other, that's what you told me before."

"Well, we were friends, too," he said defensively. "I'm *glad* she called. I just wish your mother were here. Then I could introduce the two of them and they'd be friends too."

"Hah," said Anastasia, who was quite sure that her mother had zero interest in becoming friends with Annie. "Anyway," she went on, "what do you mean, you have a date?"

He sighed. "She's coming here for dinner Friday night."

"Why on earth did you ask her to do *that?*"

Dr. Krupnik frowned. "I didn't. It was odd. She talked so much on the phone—I don't remember Annie being that talkative; she used to be a quiet sort of person—that I never had a chance to say much. Probably I would have asked her to come over to my office and I would have had a cup of coffee with her, or something—"

"Yeah, that would be okay, Dad. Not even Mom would mind—at least she wouldn't mind *much*—if you had a cup of coffee with Annie. Like for ten minutes or something. Instant coffee, maybe."

"But before I knew what was happening, she announced that she was coming for dinner Friday night. She even knew our address—she'd found it in the phone book."

"Well, that's rude, Dad. You don't just *tell* people that you're coming for dinner. I mean, what if they'd forgotten to take something out of the freezer?"

"It is sort of rude, isn't it? Funny, I don't remember Annie being rude. She was always very sweet."

"Well," said Anastasia firmly, "she's obviously turned into a rude person. So you can be rude back. You can call her and uninvite her. Tell her that you're going bowling."

"Anastasia, I've never gone bowling in my life."

Anastasia thought. "Tell her you're planning to listen to one of your complete sets of opera records, then. What's a real long opera?"

"Wagner. *The Ring*. It lasts for hours and hours and hours."

"Good. Tell her that you're listening to that Friday night, and it will take hours and hours and hours, so she can't come to dinner."

Dr. Krupnik finished his beer and set the can aside. "I can't call her. Even if I thought up a terrific excuse, I couldn't call her. She didn't tell me where she was staying."

"Oh, *rats*. She conned you, Dad."

He nodded. "I think she did."

Anastasia sat silently for a minute, thinking. Finally she said, "We'll make it a real quick dinner, then. We'll have—let's see. What's the quickest thing there is to eat?"

Sam looked up. "Hot dogs," he said. "I can eat a hot dog real fast."

"Okay. We'll have hot dogs. I'll have them all cooked when she gets here—what time is she coming? Or was she too rude to tell you?"

"Seven," her father answered.

"Okay. I'll have four hot dogs all cooked at seven o'clock. When she gets here, I'll hand her one, and we'll each have one, and we'll stand around and eat them real fast. Maybe I won't even get the mustard out. Then, the instant she finishes her last bite, we'll say, 'It was nice of you to come, Annie,' and we'll hold the door open so she'll leave. Maybe she won't even have time to take her coat off."

"But she said that we have all those years to catch up on."

"Between bites. Do it between bites. The whole thing shouldn't take longer than fifteen minutes."

Suddenly Anastasia thought of something. "Oh, RATS!" she wailed.

"What?" her father asked.

"Dad, I won't be here Friday night. I have a date."

"You have a *what?*"

"I told you, but you weren't listening because you were depressed about Annie. I have a date to go to the movies with Steve, Friday night. My very first date, *ever.*"

"Anastasia," her father said, "it's going to be bad enough when your mother finds out that Annie was here when she was in California. But if you're not here, too—well, I'm not sure what your mother will say to Annie being here when no one else was home."

"*I'll* be here," Sam pointed out cheerfully. "I don't have a date. I have chicken pox."

Anastasia and her father looked at Sam. Green ink lines crisscrossed his face, going from spot to spot.

"I guess," said Anastasia sadly, "I'm going to have to break my very first date. Talk about disaster. Probably he won't ever ask me again, he'll be so insulted."

"Anastasia," her father suggested, "why don't you invite Steve to dinner Friday night?"

Anastasia pondered that. Actually, it wasn't a bad

idea. "I don't want to just hand him a hot dog," she said. "He seems to be hungrier than that, most of the time. Even at McDonald's, he always has at least two Big Macs."

"Well, maybe we could make it a sort of dinner party. Then somehow it wouldn't seem so awkward, having Annie here."

Anastasia nodded. "It would be more chaperones."

"And tonight, when Mom calls," Dr. Krupnik said hesitantly, "I think it would be a good idea if maybe we just didn't *mention* Annie—"

"We're already not telling her I have chicken pox," Sam reminded them.

"And we're already not telling her that I'm not going to school this week, or that we're using paper plates," Anastasia said. "What can we talk about when she calls?"

"I'll talk about my trucks," Sam said, and pushed his yellow dump truck across the floor.

"And I'll ask her about recipes," Anastasia said, "since I'm in charge of the cooking."

"And *I,*" said Dr. Krupnik, "will talk about the weather, and maybe the car."

They all sighed in resignation. "We sure are

going to be boring conversationalists," Anastasia pointed out.

Anastasia dumped a can of baking powder into Sam's bath water. Sam watched with interest.

"It's burping!" he said.

And it was. The water bubbled and made small explosions here and there. "Well," Anastasia said, "I guess it's supposed to do that. Climb in, Sam. It'll make your itching go away."

Sam giggled and climbed into the tub. "I'm having a burp bath," he announced.

"Well, stay in there and soak real good. I have to make some phone calls."

Anastasia kicked off her shoes and stretched out on her parents' bed beside the telephone. First she called Steve. She knew it was poor taste for a girl to call a boy, because Ann Landers had said so, and generally Ann Landers gave pretty good advice. But she called Steve anyway.

"Well," Steve said, after Anastasia had explained (although she didn't go into detail about Annie), "I guess I could come for dinner. What're you having for food?"

Anastasia was quite sure that Ann Landers would consider that a rude response. But she didn't want to louse up her date with Steve by commenting on his manners. And she knew that food was important to Steve; he always gave special instructions for his Big Macs.

"I don't know yet. But it'll be good. I'm going to spend the rest of the week preparing for Friday night, since I can't go to school anyway. Did anything interesting happen in school today?"

"Yeah," Steve said, "you got a new name. Anachronism. Anachronism Krupnik."

"Thanks a *lot*. What does it mean?"

Steve chortled. "Look it up in your dictionary," he said, using the English teacher's high-pitched voice. "Use it three times and it will be yours."

Anastasia glowered. "I'll see you on Friday night," she said, "at seven."

"Sure," Steve replied before he hung up.

Anastasia lay on the bed, listening to Sam singing a song he had just composed about burping as he splashed in the tub. It was weird, thought Anastasia, her very first date. She liked the *idea* of it. But Steve was obnoxious. Somehow it wasn't what she had envisioned. Being picked up in a taxi, having a corsage pinned to the shoulder of a shimmering gown, listening to violin music in a dimly lit restaurant, and clinking champagne glasses together while gazing into each other's eyes was what she had always daydreamed about. "What're you having for food?" didn't seem to fit into her daydream. "Anachro—" What was that word? It didn't fit, either. "Darling" was what you should be called on your daydream date.

Then she remembered something that her mother had once told her. Her mother had said that people have to make their own daydreams come true.

Anastasia tucked that away in her mind to think about some more. She still had three days left before her first date. If she worked at it, maybe she could create the scene that she had daydreamed. Also, she would have to create a new housekeeping schedule in order to prepare.

She reached for the phone again and called Daphne. It was important, in talking to Daphne, to be supercool. After some casual chat about school ("Marlene Braverman has mono," Daphne announced; "Boooring," Anastasia replied), she said, "I gotta go. I have to call Sonya and Meredith, still. Oh, by the way, I have a date Friday night."

Gleefully she heard Daphne's stifled gasp. Daphne had been hanging around with Eddie Fox all year, but they had never had a real date.

Then Daphne pulled herself together. "With who?" she asked in a bored voice.

"Whom, Daph," Anastasia corrected. "With *whom*. It's with Steve."

"That turkey."

"Yeah," yawned Anastasia.

Next she called Sonya. You didn't have to be supercool with Sonya. Sonya was constitutionally incapable of being supercool. Sonya's chubby face turned bright pink when she was excited, and she overflowed with excitement most of the time.

"Guess what, Sonya!" Anastasia squealed into the phone. "Steve called and asked me for a date!"

There was a shriek and a thump on the other end of the telephone. Anastasia waited, grinning.

"Here I am again," Sonya announced breathlessly. "I fell on the floor in a faint. You are sooooo lucky, Anastasia! That jerk Norman Berkowitz will probably *never* ask me for a date, at least not until I lose ten pounds and have a whole new body with sex appeal. And right at this very instant I'm eating a Nestlé Crunch bar."

"I thought you were on a diet."

"I am. But it makes me hungry."

"Use willpower, Sonya," Anastasia said.

She could hear the rustle of a candy bar wrapper over the phone. "There," Sonya told her. "I wrapped the rest of it up. I *am* going to use willpower, Anastasia. Call me tomorrow night and remind me. I wish you could come to school so you could remind me at lunch."

"Throw the rest of it away, Sonya. Right this instant."

There was a silence. "Well," Sonya said, "I'll put it in the freezer, behind the hamburger. I'm not strong enough yet to actually throw it away."

Anastasia was in the middle of her third phone call, to Meredith, when Sam came shivering in from the bathroom, wrapped in a towel. Anastasia said a hurried goodbye and turned to her brother.

"The water got cold," Sam explained. "And it stopped burping."

"It didn't get the green lines off," Anastasia said,

examining him. "Those must be indelible markers. But at least it cured your itching, didn't it?"

"No," Sam said mournfully. "I still itch."

Anastasia sighed. "I bet it was baking *soda* I was supposed to use. Well, try not to scratch, Sam. We'll try baking soda tomorrow."

She combed Sam's damp hair — carefully, because his head was covered with chicken pox — and put his pajamas on. They found their father in the study, listening to music and reading the newspaper.

"It's almost time for Mom to call," Anastasia said, looking at her watch. "You stay here, Dad, and I'll be by the phone in the kitchen, and Sam, you go up by the phone in Mom and Dad's room, so we can all talk to her.

"But remember, everybody," she added, "there are certain things that we don't mention."

"Annie," her father said.

"Chicken pox," Sam said.

"Or paper plates," Anastasia said. "Can you remember that, Sam? We'll have a *blood oath* that we won't mention anything that might upset Mom."

"Yeah," Sam said with delight. "Bludoth."

The telephone rang at that moment, and Sam and

Anastasia dashed to their extensions while their father answered.

"I'm exhausted," Mrs. Krupnik was saying when Anastasia got to the phone, "but it's such fun. Everybody's so nice, and so helpful—"

"Do they glitter?" Anastasia asked. "I'm on the extension in the kitchen," she explained. "Sam's upstairs. Say hi, Sam."

"Hi, Mom," Sam said. "I'm only going to talk about trucks."

Their mother laughed. "I really miss you guys," she said. "Some people seem to glitter a little, Anastasia. But mostly they're just ordinary. And my clothes seem to be fine."

"That's a relief. I was really worried about that, Mom."

"But I want to hear about *you*," Mrs. Krupnik said. "Is everything going okay? How's the housekeeping schedule working?"

"The weather wasn't bad today," said their father. "And the car is okay."

"How was nursery school today, Sam? Is it fun going for a full day?" his mother asked.

"Blood oath, Sam," muttered Anastasia into the phone.

"I'm only going to talk about trucks," Sam said.

Mrs. Krupnik laughed. "Did you play with trucks at school today?"

Sam was silent for a minute. "Blood oath, Sam," Anastasia murmured.

"The yellow dump truck goes *'Rrrrrrrr,'*" Sam said.

"You should see the trucks in California," Mrs. Krupnik said. "Boy, do they speed along the freeways!"

"How's the weather out there?" asked Dr. Krupnik.

"Gorgeous. Sunny and warm. My hotel has a pool, and of course I'm too busy all day to use it, but there are a lot of people who lie around the pool all day—glittering, I think, Anastasia. How's the food holding out, by the way? Don't forget you can call the store and have things delivered if you need anything. What did you have for dinner tonight?"

"Chicken," said Dr. Krupnik.

"Hamburger," said Anastasia at the same moment.

"Hot dogs," said Sam along with them.

But apparently Mrs. Krupnik didn't notice. "They're taking me out to dinner tonight," she went on. "It's three hours earlier here, remember? So I've just finished work and I'm getting ready to go out to dinner. You guys ought to treat yourselves to a dinner out, too — maybe Friday night, at the end of the week," she suggested.

"Well, ah," began Dr. Krupnik.

"Bludoth, Daddy," muttered Sam.

"What was that?" asked Mrs. Krupnik. "I couldn't hear what Sam said."

Sam said, "I'm only talking about trucks."

"You know what?" Mrs. Krupnik went on cheerfully. "There are palm trees everywhere out here. It almost looks like that painting in the living room, you know that one I sometimes wish you would throw away, Myron? It looks like that scene. Where is it that Annie lives?"

Anastasia covered the mouthpiece of the kitchen phone with her hand and yelled toward the study: "BLOOD OATH, DAD!"

She put her ear back to the phone and heard her father mumble, "Guatemala."

"Right. Well, I ought to hang up because I have to change my clothes. It's just about your bedtime there in Massachusetts, Sam. Have you had your bath?"

"Yeah," said Sam, "I had a burping bath with baking—"

"Blood oath, Sam!" Anastasia and her father roared together into the phone.

"This is an odd connection," Mrs. Krupnik said. "But even so, it's great hearing your voices and knowing that everything's okay." She made some kissing noises into the phone. "Love you all," she said.

When everyone had hung up, Anastasia went back to the study. Her father was sprawled on the couch, looking drained and miserable. "I'm a nervous wreck," he announced. "A basket case."

"Hang in there, Dad," said Anastasia. "Only eight more days to go till Mom gets home."

Sam came down the stairs and appeared in the doorway of the study. He looked puzzled. "Anastasia," he asked, "what *is* a bludoth?"

Krupnik Housekeeping Schedule for Week with First Date

Version 5

7:00 A.M.   Myron gets up, makes his own breakfast,
            leaves.

LATER Other people get up when they feel like it, have
breakfast.

Anastasia feeds Frank Goldfish.
Take something out of freezer for dinner.

Anastasia begins planning for Friday night.
   Candles.
   Flowers.
   Music.

Menu for dinner party.
   Anastasia reads through old issues of <u>Cosmopolitan</u>
magazine which are hidden under her bed, looking for
suggestions for date/dinner and for romantic recipes.

Call store and have food delivered. Don't forget
baking soda.

DURING DAY, sometime. Anastasia and Sam find something
in the refrigerator for lunch.

Anastasia practices romantic conversation for date,
also looks through Katherine's make-up and tries out
various combinations of things. Also thinks about what
to wear for date.

Sam plays all day, and watches TV, and has a couple of
baths with baking soda if he itches.

5:00 P.M.   Myron comes home and they make dinner.

*** Things like vacuuming, laundry, and window-washing
can all wait till after Friday.

six

$\mathcal{N}$ow it was interesting and exciting, all of a sudden, being in charge of a house. There was laundry, but Anastasia didn't do it. There were dirty pots and pans in the sink, but she didn't wash them. Those things didn't seem important anymore. The important thing was that she had three days to make a daydream come true: the daydream of her very first date.

On Wednesday morning, she looked through the drawers in the pantry and found a pair of purple candles. High on a shelf she found a pair of silver candlesticks.

One of the articles she had read—the one called "Creating a Romantic Evening"—had recommended a color scheme. Purple was not one of Anastasia's favorite colors. In fact, she had always despised purple. But the article had rated colors according to romance, and purple had rated very highly. Purple, the article said, was the color of passion.

All right, thought Anastasia when she found the two purple candles, passion it is.

She put the candles into the candlesticks and arranged the pair in the center of the dining room table, for a tryout. It didn't look very passionate. In fact, Anastasia decided, it looked stupid. But maybe that was because there was a stack of Sam's coloring books on the table, and Sam's crayons and her father's pipe, in an ashtray, and Anastasia's old blue sweatshirt was hanging on the back of one of the dining room chairs.

She removed all of those things and looked at the table again. It still didn't look very passionate. It needed a tablecloth.

Anastasia went to the linen closet and poked through the stacks of things that her mother stored there. There was an orange and white striped plastic tablecloth, which they used in the summer when they ate on the picnic table in the yard. Obviously that wouldn't do.

But the only other tablecloth was white. White was not a passionate color. Even the article pointed that out; it had rated white very low on the passion scale.

She decided to think some more about table-cloths. There would be some solution, she knew; she only had to think of it.

She glanced through the article again and read what it said about flowers. There had to be flowers. Flowers were a *must* for a romantic evening.

But the yard around the house was covered with snow. She would have to think more, to come up with a solution to the flower problem.

Music. That was essential too, but that would be easy. Her father's record collection covered almost an entire wall in the study, and it was arranged alphabetically. The article listed several extremely romantic pieces of music, and she found one with no trouble at all: Rachmaninoff's Second Piano Concerto. She put it on the stereo and listened for a few minutes. *Perfect*. It was so romantic — so *passionate* — that Anastasia almost passed out listening to it. No *wonder* she'd never heard it before; her father had probably been saving it until she was old enough to understand passion.

And now, of course, she was. Now she was having her first date.

Sam sauntered into the dining room, in his pajamas, while Anastasia was still looking at the table with its two purple candles.

"You shouldn't be barefoot, Sam," Anastasia said. "You'll catch cold."

"No, I won't," Sam said. "I have chicken pox instead. When do I get my bath in that other stuff, so I won't itch?"

"In a minute, after I figure this out."

"Figure what out?"

"How to create a purple tablecloth. All we have is this white one."

"You could color it," Sam suggested, and fished a purple crayon out of the coffee can of crayons that Anastasia had taken off the table.

"It wouldn't work. Thanks, Sam, but that's not a good solution." Suddenly she thought of something. The word *solution* had been the key. "I'll dye it!" Anastasia said. "They have all these bottles of dye at the grocery store, and when I call in the order of groceries to be delivered, I'll have them send some purple dye!"

"I itch," said Sam.

"Okay. Come on and I'll fix you a bath with baking soda in it."

Sam trotted behind Anastasia while she went to the kitchen and found the box of baking soda. This time she looked at what was written on the box. "Hey," she said with satisfaction, "look at that. It says, right on the box, 'Soothes minor skin irritations.' If I'd read the boxes yesterday, I wouldn't have used the wrong stuff last night."

"But then," Sam pointed out as he followed her up the stairs to the bathroom, "I wouldn't have had that burping bath."

"True." Anastasia emptied the box of baking soda into the tub and turned the water on. When the bathtub was full she stripped Sam's pajamas off and helped him in. "Now soak for a while," she said, and handed him some plastic boats, "while I call the grocery store."

At the kitchen telephone, Anastasia consulted the cookbook that she had studied after breakfast. Her magazine article had suggested veal as a romantic dinner, so she had found a veal recipe called Ragout de Veau aux Champignons. Even the name sounded passionate. It looked somewhat complicated, but she had three days to work on it, she figured, and undoubtedly she could master it in that time.

"Hi, Mr. Fortunato," she said when the grocer answered the phone. "It's Anastasia Krupnik. I'm in charge because my mother's away, so I want to order some stuff and have it delivered."

"Sure thing," he said. "Your mama told me you might be calling. What do you need?"

Anastasia looked at the recipe. "Three pounds of boneless lean veal cut into one-and-a-half-inch chunks," she said. "Wait a minute, Mr. Fortunato; it says 'see notes preceding recipe.'"

"Take your time."

Anastasia flipped the page back and read the notes. "The notes say that if your meat is boneless you should tie some chopped veal marrow and knucklebones in cheesecloth and simmer them with the meat," she told the grocer.

"So you want veal marrow and knucklebones?" he asked.

"Yeah, I guess so. Do you have cheesecloth?"

"Nope."

"Well, I'll find some around the house. Okay; let me go back to the recipe. Salt, pepper, flour: I have all of that. I need olive oil."

"Okay. Olive oil. What else?"

"Dry white wine."

"This is quite a meal you're planning, Anastasia," commented Mr. Fortunato.

"It's called Ragout de Veau aux Champignons. I probably didn't pronounce it right. Also, Mr. Fortunato, just so you won't get in trouble with the law or anything—I'm not going to drink that wine. I'm only thirteen. It goes in with the veal, to cook."

"Fine. I've got some nice dry wines here. What else?"

"Tarragon, basil, oregano, bay leaf, garlic, and two tomatoes."

"Hold it," said Mr. Fortunato, "I can't write that fast." Anastasia waited.

"Okay," the grocer said. "What else?"

"Eight ounces of fresh mushrooms, and some parsley, and some heavy cream."

"Is that it?" he asked.

"Almost. I also want—Let me think a minute."

Anastasia calculated in her head. If Sam had de-itching baths three times a day, and if his chicken pox lasted, as the doctor had said it would, a week or more ... "I want twenty-one boxes of baking soda."

"*Twenty-one boxes of baking soda?*"

"Yes. And a bottle of purple dye."

There was a moment of silence. "That's going to be a very interesting dinner you're having, Anastasia," Mr. Fortunato said. "The boy'll bring everything over in a couple of hours. And I'll just add it to your mama's bill."

"Thanks," said Anastasia, and she hung up. She grinned. It was *neat,* she thought happily, being in charge of a house—especially if you had a romantic dinner to prepare.

Sam came down the stairs, naked. "I dried myself," he said. "And I don't itch anymore. And look—I did all my green lines over, in purple."

"You look grotesque, Sam," Anastasia said. "But at least you'll match my color scheme."

By late afternoon, Anastasia had put all of the groceries away except the bottle of purple dye. She was reading the directions on the bottle when there was a knock at the back door.

"Hi, you guys!" she said in delight when she opened the door and saw Sonya and Meredith standing there.

"We brought you your homework assignments and your books," Sonya announced, "but we can't come in. *I* could come in, because I've had chicken pox, but Meredith's mom can't remember if she's had chicken pox, so she can't come in, and I promised I wouldn't leave her standing out here all alone."

"I think I had it," Meredith explained, "because I remember itching a lot, but my mother thinks maybe what I remember is poison ivy."

Anastasia took the books and made a face. "I'm not going to have time to do homework," she said. "I don't know how my mom ever finds time to do her illustrating. It takes all day just to take care of a house. Keep that in mind, you guys, when you start thinking about getting married. Look for a rich husband so you can have servants."

"Speaking of getting married," Sonya said, giggling, "tell us more about your date with Steve."

"Well, he wanted to take me to the mov—ah, to the theater," Anastasia explained. "But I decided it would be better to have a romantic dinner date. So he's coming here, and I'm fixing a gourmet dinner, with candles and everything."

She had already decided not to tell anyone—even her best friends—about Annie.

"But, Anastasia," Meredith said in her very practical voice, "you don't know how to cook a gourmet dinner. You even burned the English muffins that time you slept over at my house."

"That's what *books* are for, Meredith," Anastasia pointed out. "I have this book—actually, it's my mom's—called *Mastering the Art of French Cooking*. I've been reading it practically all day. Anyway, that time at your house? I wasn't *into* cooking, then."

"Don't even tell me what you're going to cook for your gourmet dinner," Sonya said, "because it'll make me hungry. All I had for lunch was an apple and two glasses of water. Practically zero calories."

"What're you going to wear?" Meredith asked.

"I don't know. I'm going to look through my mom's clothes and see if I can find something to borrow. It has to be purple. My color scheme is purple. Hey—that reminds me. I need some flowers. Do you guys know where I could find some flowers?"

They all glanced out into the snow-covered yard.

"There aren't any flowers this time of year," Sonya pointed out. "You'll have to use fake flowers."

"My sister has some fake flowers in her room," Meredith said. "Big ones, made of crepe paper. You want me to steal them for you?"

Anastasia thought about that. Crepe paper flowers didn't sound very romantic. She shook her head. "I don't think so. Only in an emergency. I'll call you if I need them."

Meredith sighed, and her breath made a puff of steam in the cold winter air. "You know, Anastasia," she said wistfully, "of the four of us—you, me, Sonya, and Daphne—you're the very first one to get into a real romance, with a dinner date and everything. We're all really jealous. You know how supercool Daph pretends to be? Well, even Daphne confessed during lunch that she wished she would have a real date, like you, instead of just yelling insults back and forth with Eddie at McDonald's every Saturday."

Anastasia nodded sympathetically. "The thing is, Steve just happened to become mature a little sooner than the other seventh grade guys. They'll catch up pretty soon. Then we'll *all* have romantic dates every weekend."

She turned to Sonya. "Even Norman Berkowitz will become mature, Sonya. You wait."

Sonya stamped her feet up and down on the back steps. "I'm freezing," she announced. "My body chemistry is all screwed up since I haven't been eating anything. My body is living on my fat, and I'm freezing. My fat used to keep me warm."

"You're freezing because it's cold out," Meredith told her. "I'm freezing, too, and I ate two whole lunches—mine and yours."

"You'd better go," Anastasia said. "I'm freezing, standing here with the door open. Thanks for coming over."

She waved as her friends headed down the driveway, toward the street. Then she went back to the kitchen to write out her schedule for the next day. The bulletin board was becoming cluttered with revised schedules. But there was so much to do when you had a romantic date. She wondered how movie actresses and models managed—they had romantic dates *every night.*

After Sam was in bed and Dr. Krupnik was in the study reading the paper, Anastasia went to her parents' room and looked through the drawer where her mother kept makeup. Mrs. Krupnik didn't actually *wear* makeup very often; she said it made her face itch. But she had quite an assortment of things. Some of them, she had told Anastasia, were probably twenty years old.

Anastasia looked for everything that was purple.

Then she lined it all up on the table in front of the mirror and began the application.

First she took off her glasses and put deep purple eye shadow across her eyelids. With her glasses back on, though, she could hardly see it. If only she didn't have to wear glasses, Anastasia thought. Usually she liked the intellectual look that her glasses gave her—but for a passionate evening, she didn't want to look intellectual.

Maybe she could leave her glasses off on Friday evening. But when she removed them, experimentally, she realized once again that everything was a blur. It would never work. She wouldn't even be able to serve dinner. She would bump into the table, and she would spill things.

She sighed, and added more of the purple eye shadow so that it would show under the rims of her glasses.

There was no purple rouge, but she used the deepest red she could find, and smeared circles across her cheeks. Then she carefully applied purplish red lipstick, going slightly beyond the borders of her lips to give herself a mature, passionate look.

She opened her mother's jewelry box and found, to her delight, a pair of dangly earrings with some small purple stones. Wincing, she screwed them tightly onto her earlobes. Good grief. No *wonder* her mother never wore those earrings; they were excruciating.

Still, when she looked at herself in the mirror, tilting her head from side to side so that the earrings moved and jangled, the effect was terrific.

I *glitter,* Anastasia thought.

But the hair, she thought despondently. The hair stinks.

She brushed her long straight hair, bunched it up in her hand, and twisted it onto the top of her head. Firmly she adhered it there with bobby pins. That hurt, too. In fact, she was now in almost unbearable pain, both in her earlobes and on the top of her head.

But it's worth it, she thought, looking in the mirror at her new self, purple with makeup, glittering in the ears, and minus the long mane of tangled hair. I'm a new person. A new sophisticated, mature, *passionate* person.

Maybe I should show Dad, she thought.

No. Better to surprise him, when I appear on Friday night.

Quickly she undid her hair, removed the earrings, and went to the bathroom to wash off the makeup. A pink washcloth was ruined; she tossed it into the laundry hamper. She gathered up the makeup, the earrings, and the bobby pins to take them to her room. As an afterthought, she looked in the medicine cabinet and added a bottle of aspirin to her load. I may need that, she thought, to counteract the pain when I put on those earrings and bobby pins again.

>< >< ><

Scrubbed, brushed, and in her pajamas and bath-robe, Anastasia went down to the study. Her father had started a fire in the fireplace, and there was music playing on the stereo. He looked up from the book he was reading when Anastasia came in.

"I want to talk to you, Dad," she said.

"Guess what," he said. "Some intruder was here. Someone with no taste."

"What do you mean? No one was here all day except me and Sam. Meredith and Sonya stopped by with my homework, but they didn't come in. Anyway, they have great taste. You should see the new sweatshirt Meredith has—PUNK CITY is written across the front, in rhinestones."

Dr. Krupnik laughed. "I'll argue that one with you some other time," he said, "in about five years. No, look; here's what I meant. Look what I found on the stereo."

He picked up the Rachmaninoff album and displayed it with a look of disdain.

"Dad, *I* was playing that. It's *great*."

"Anastasia, I wish you'd learn to appreciate Bach. Rachmaninoff is *schmaltzy*."

Anastasia flopped on the couch beside him. "Wouldn't you say that it's romantic, Dad? I read in a magazine that that record is romantic, and so I tried it out, and it *is*. At least I thought so. It almost made me faint, listening to it."

"*Faint?* Did you forget to eat lunch?"

Anastasia thought. "Well, yes, I guess I did forget to eat lunch. I fed Sam, though. I gave him scrambled eggs."

Her father put the album back down. "Try to remember to eat, Anastasia. It's important, especially at your age. You're a growing girl."

"Dad, that's sort of what I want to talk to you about. About the fact that I'm growing up, and having a date Friday night and all that. And I want to talk to you, ah, about passion."

Her father put his book down. He lit his pipe. "About passion?" he asked, after he got the pipe going. "Help! Where's your mother? I need your mother. This is the kind of conversation thirteen-year-old girls are supposed to have with their *mothers*."

Anastasia giggled. "Don't panic," she said reassuringly. "It's just that I'm kind of worried about you."

"About me?"

"I mean about you and Friday night. The problem is this: it's my very first date, as you know, and that's important, and I think I'm being a pretty good sport about not going to the movies so that I can be a chaperone for you and Annie—"

"'Good sport' isn't the term for it, Anastasia. You're a savior. You've absolutely saved my life, and my mental health, and my reputation. I was a nervous wreck, anticipating the evening with Annie. But look at me now: calm, cool. I'm not even worried about seeing Annie now, because of you. It won't be any big deal."

"But you see, I'm planning a passionate evening."

"You're planning a *what?*"

"I have this magazine article that tells about how to plan a dinner date, and so I'm following its directions on how to make it romantic, and I have a color scheme and all, and that's why I got that record out, because the article said it was passionate."

Dr. Krupnik glanced at the record with a wry look. "Oh," he said.

"But I have several problems. One is that I have to have flowers, and I don't have flowers."

"Well," said her father, "I can solve that one for

you. There's a flower shop in Harvard Square. I'll bring home some flowers on Friday."

"Purple," Anastasia said.

"Purple?"

"Yeah, because that's my color scheme. Purple is supposed to be a passionate color."

"Just exactly how passionate is this evening supposed to be?" her father asked, with his forehead furrowed. "I thought it was going to be a casual dinner."

"Well, I want to discuss that in a minute. But first, I have another problem. Do you know what cheesecloth is?"

"No. Sometimes expensive cheese comes wrapped in a sort of disgusting clothlike stuff. Is that cheesecloth?"

"I don't know. But I need some. Do you think we have any?"

"Hold it. I *do* know how to do research. Hand me the dictionary, Anastasia."

She took the thick red volume from the bookcase and gave it to her father.

He flipped through the pages until he found the right one. "Here," he said. "'Cheesecloth. A coarse cotton gauze.'"

"Gauze? Like a bandage?"

"I guess so."

"I bet we have bandages. From the time Sam fell out the window last summer and hurt his head. Mom had to change his bandages. I think there are some left over, in the bathroom closet. Good. That's solved. Now we can talk about passion."

Dr. Krupnik groaned and put the dictionary on the floor. "I was afraid you were going to say that."

"Here's the problem. You and Annie are going to be there—"

"And Sam. Don't forget Sam, and Steve. I need all the chaperones I can get."

"Okay, but what I'm talking about is you and Annie. Now, as I told you, I'm going to have all this romantic stuff, the purple color scheme, and that record, and the French food, and the candles. But that's for me and Steve. I don't want *you* to be affected by it. I don't want you and Annie to start feeling romantic or anything. I thought about asking you to eat in the kitchen, with the fluorescent light on, but—"

Her father laughed. "Anastasia, you needn't worry about that. We'll eat in the passionately purple dining room, but frankly, all I'm planning to do is ask

Annie about her life in Guatemala, and then I'll brag a bit about Katherine and my kids, and then she'll leave. And as for the romantic music—well, it may make you faint with passion, but frankly, it turns my stomach. So I'll probably have to excuse myself several times to throw up."

"Good. That's very unromantic. I hope Annie throws up, too.

"My only other problem is one that I guess you can't solve," Anastasia went on with resignation.

"What's that? Try me."

"Promise you won't tell Daphne, or Sonya, or Meredith."

Her father promised.

"Well, with all this passion and romance and my first date and everything, frankly, I have a horrible feeling that Steve Harvey is the wrong person."

"But you said he was your boyfriend."

"He *is*, but he's not at all romantic. He's so adolescent."

"Well, of course he's adolescent, Anastasia. He's thirteen years old."

"Yeah." Anastasia sighed. "Thirteen-year-old boys

are so gross. I wish my first date was with Laurence Olivier. *That* would be romantic."

Her father almost choked on the stem of his pipe. "Laurence Olivier's probably eighty years old!" he said.

"He is *not*. I watch *Wuthering Heights* every time they show it on TV, and Laurence Olivier is just the right age for passion."

"Anastasia, they made that movie *years* ago. That movie's almost as old as I am!"

"It *is?*" Anastasia asked angrily. "Oh, *rats!* That's *cheating!* Now I have to get a whole new fantasy!"

Her father yawned and tapped the ashes from his pipe into the ashtray. "Do me a favor, Anastasia," he said. "Wait till next week. I think we have enough to handle right now."

Krupnik Housekeeping Schedule
in Preparation for Romantic Evening

Version 6

Read recipe for Ragout de Veau aux Champignons in
Mastering the Art of French Cooking. Read it a lot. Try
to figure out things like cheesecloth.

Create purple tablecloth.

Flowers. Dad will take care of flowers on Friday.

Candles and candlesticks — DONE.

Give Sam baking soda bath.

Romantic music — DONE. READY on stereo.

Give Sam baking soda bath #2.

Practice make-up. Try to think of exercise which will
strengthen earlobes.

Practice conversation. Think up mature topics.

Baking soda bath #3.

FORGET ENTIRELY: Beds, laundry, dishes, vacuuming,
windows, etc. These things are not important this week.

seven

On Thursday morning Anastasia realized that her father, despite his insistence that he was no longer upset about the coming evening with Annie, was actually very, very nervous. Panic-stricken, in fact. Anastasia had never seen her father panic-stricken before. Always, in the midst of dire emergencies and horrendous catastrophes, her father had remained calm.

When Sam had fallen out of the second-story window—right on his head—last summer, her father had not only called the ambulance but had also ridden in it with Sam to the hospital.

When Anastasia's eleven gerbils had escaped from their cage and disappeared all over the house, her father had just chuckled and helped Anastasia and Sam collect the wiggling little rodents and return them to captivity.

When a water pipe had burst in their basement, sending a geyser as big as Old Faithful right across the Ping-Pong table with such force that it knocked over the net, her father had simply gone to the telephone very calmly and called the plumber.

But now, on Thursday morning, her father came down to the kitchen with shaving cream on his neck. When Sam pointed it out, Dr. Krupnik looked startled, and went back up to the bathroom to finish shaving.

When he reappeared, he was in his stocking feet.

"Dad, where are your shoes?" Anastasia asked.

"Shoes?" her father said, and looked at his feet. "Oh yes, shoes." And he went back upstairs to find his shoes.

When the telephone rang, Dr. Krupnik jumped as if he had heard a shot. "You answer it, Anastasia," he said in a nervous voice.

Anastasia was already up from the table. "Hello," she said, and then listened to the salesman on the other end. "Just a minute," she said.

"Dad? Are you interested in taking tap-dancing lessons? It's a special discount offer. The first lesson's absolutely free."

"Taking what? Tap-dancing lessons? I don't know. Maybe. I guess—Well, no, I don't think so. But I can't decide." Her father stared at her.

"I don't think you are. You hate dancing," Anastasia pointed out.

"Yes, right. I hate dancing," her father said in the same confused voice.

"I like to dance," said Sam, and he twirled around the kitchen. "But I don't want to take dancing lessons. I want to take karate lessons."

"Maybe *I* should take tap-dancing lessons," Anastasia said. She tried tap-dancing across the floor, but her hiking boots were too heavy, and one was untied. She tripped and stumbled against the refrigerator. Rubbing her bruised hip, she went back to the phone.

"Would you call back later?" she asked politely. "I can't decide right now."

Her father stood up, put on his coat, and started out the door. "I have to go," he said. "I'm teaching a class at nine. I'm giving a quiz on—"

He stood still, and thought. "I'm giving a quiz on something," he said. "I can't remember what."

Anastasia and Sam stared as he went out without saying goodbye. They watched through the window as he went to the garage, turned, and came back.

He laughed apologetically when he reappeared in the kitchen. "Forgot my briefcase," he said, and picked up the pile of schoolbooks that Meredith and Sonya had brought the afternoon before.

Anastasia stopped him in the open door. She took her math and history books gently from his arm and replaced them with his briefcase. He left again, and after a moment they saw the car back out, spewing smoke, and then disappear down the street.

"Daddy's weird today," Sam said. "Can I make a salad bar out of my oatmeal?"

"Sure."

Sam went to the cupboard and gazed at the contents. Then he removed some raisins, some peanuts, some brown sugar, some shredded coconut, a crumbled Ginger Snap, and some instant coffee. Carefully he added each ingredient to his oatmeal, picked up his spoon, and began to eat.

>< >< ><

"Okay," Anastasia said aloud to herself after she had added the breakfast dishes to the pile of dirty things in the sink, "now I have to get organized.

"First I'll do the tablecloth." She glanced again at the directions on the bottle of dye. She turned the water on in the washing machine, opened the bottle, and dumped the contents in.

"Yuck," she said, peering in after it. "It looks *black*." Cautiously she reached in, dipped one fingertip into the water, and examined the color when she took it out. "Good. It's purple." She unfolded the white tablecloth, added it to the machine, and closed the lid.

"Next, the Ragout de Veau aux Champignons." She opened the cookbook to the correct page and re-read the beginning of the recipe to confirm what she had read before: that it was okay to make it a day in advance.

"'Dry the veal on paper towels,'" she read. "Okay." She took the package of veal Mr. Fortunato had sent, opened it, and made a face. "I didn't know it would be *pink*," she muttered.

Sam looked up from the kitchen table, where he was coloring a picture. "Pink's a good color," he said. "I think I might color this elephant pink."

Anastasia ignored him. Pink was a good color, she thought, maybe for underwear or something, but it looked kind of gross when it was raw meat. It looked suspiciously like newborn gerbils. She pulled some paper towels from the roller and dried the veal.

"'Salt and pepper,'" she read, and sprinkled the meat with salt and pepper. "Some people think gourmet cooking is hard," she confided to Sam, "but that's just because they haven't tried it. If you follow the directions, it's easy.

"Now," she said, and read some more from the recipe, "'roll it in flour.' How on earth do you roll it in flour?"

Sam didn't answer. His tongue was between his teeth, and he was busily coloring a picture of an elephant.

Anastasia shrugged. She dumped some flour into a bowl, and rolled the pieces of veal, one at a time. In a corner of the kitchen, the washing machine was churning away.

"There," said Anastasia when all of the pieces of veal were covered with flour. "Now. 'Heat oil in a pan until hot but not smoking.' Simple."

She opened the bottle of olive oil, but couldn't find a pan.

"Rats," she said when she realized that all of the pans were in the sink. She fished one out, examined it, and decided that it needed washing. It would have been okay for another batch of hamburgers; but for a gourmet dinner, it needed washing. Hastily she washed it, added oil, and put it on the stove to heat.

"Timing is the secret to good cooking," Anastasia told Sam. "Like right now, while the veal is browning in that pan, I have to cook the onions in a different pan, at the same time. Rats. I don't *have* another pan." She sighed, and went to the sink to wash a second pan.

The first pan began to smoke. Hastily, Anastasia turned the heat down and added the veal. She went back to the sink and finished washing the second pan.

"Do you think it's okay for an elephant to have one orange ear and one blue ear?" asked Sam.

"Sure." Anastasia added oil to the second pan and put it on the stove.

"Whoops," she said, "I forgot to chop the onion." Quickly she found a knife in the sink, examined it, decided it could survive without being washed, and began to chop an onion. "People who wear glasses, like me, Sam," she said, "are really lucky because they can chop onions without crying. The glasses protect their eyes."

"That other pan is smoking," Sam said.

Anastasia ran to the stove, turned the heat down, and finished chopping the onion. She put it into the second pan.

"Timing is the key," she said again.

The telephone rang.

"This is Ralph at the Good Times Dance Studio again," the man said. "You asked me to call you back. Have you thought about the tap-dancing offer? First lesson's absolutely free."

"Well, I've sort of been thinking about it. But I have some questions. Is it important to be graceful? I don't seem to be a very graceful person. I bump into stuff a lot, and knock things over. Right when I was talking to you before, I tried dancing across the kitchen, and I bumped into the handle on the refrigerator door."

"Sounds as if you're just the right kind of person for dancing lessons," the man said. "Dance lessons turn an awkward person into a graceful person, give self-confidence, increase poise."

"Well, I *could* use an increase in poise. And I'm not real big on self-confidence, but my mother said that self-confidence is something that increases naturally with age."

"We've had students who arrived for their first lesson absolutely quaking with shyness, and by the end of only *one* lesson, their inhibitions were lessened, their natural grace was enhanced — did I tell you that the first lesson is free?"

"Yeah. Oh, HOLD IT! My onions are burning! Call me back later, would you?"

Anastasia hung up the phone and ran to the stove to rescue her onions.

She scraped at the bottom of the pan with a spatula. "Only the bottom ones are burned," she said. "And actually, I *like* the taste of burned onions."

"Me too," said Sam.

"Good. Then it doesn't matter that they got burned. The meat looks okay." Anastasia stirred the browning veal with a wooden spoon. "In fact, it looks much better, now that it's not pink."

She read the next part of the recipe. "Now I add

the veal to the onions, and I put the wine into the veal pan and mix it with the meat juices. Heck, that's simple. I wonder why people think gourmet cooking is hard."

She transferred the meat to the pan where the onions were. She got out the bottle of wine that Mr. Fortunato had sent.

In the corner of the kitchen, the washing machine clicked and changed from WASH to RINSE. Anastasia examined the bottle of wine. "Good," she said, "right on the label it says 'extra dry.' Just what the recipe wants." She tried to remove the cap from the bottle.

"That's weird," she said to Sam. "This cap won't unscrew."

Sam glanced over. "Daddy uses that special thing," he said.

"*What* special thing?"

Sam sighed, climbed out of his chair, and went to the top drawer of the cupboard. He took something out, handed it to Anastasia, and went back to his elephant picture.

Anastasia turned it over and over in her hands. Her index finger, she noticed, was still purple. "What is this thing, Sam?" she asked. "It looks like a lethal weapon. How does it work?"

Sam shrugged. "I don't know." He began to color the elephant's left leg green.

The telephone rang. Anastasia answered it with the weapon in her hand.

"Did you save your onions?" the man asked. "This is Ralph, at the Good Times Dance Studio, calling back."

"Yeah, the onions are okay," Anastasia said. "But I'm glad you called. Do you know how to open a bottle of wine?"

"Sure. Do you have a corkscrew?"

"Is that the thing with a curly metal part, and two weird handles on the sides?"

"Right."

"Well, I've got one right here. How does it work?"

"You'll need both hands," said the man. "Can you wedge the phone on your shoulder?"

"Yeah." Anastasia wedged the phone between her ear and her shoulder, and followed Ralph's instructions carefully. She screwed the corkscrew into the cork, and then carefully lowered the two raised handles. With a squishy *pop,* the cork emerged.

"Hey, that's neat!" she said to the man on the phone. "Thank you. I bet I could do it all by myself next time."

"See how with proper instruction, your self-confidence increases? The same thing is true, of course, with tap-dancing lessons."

"Yeah, well, listen, I don't feel ready to make a decision about tap-dancing when I'm in the middle of all this gourmet cooking. Could you call me back in about an hour?"

"Will do," Ralph said, and hung up.

Anastasia added a cup of wine to the pan the veal had cooked in; she swished it around with the remaining scraps of meat, and then added the mixture to the veal and onions, as the recipe instructed. Carefully she added the herbs, tomatoes, and a canful of chicken broth.

"Now," she announced, "this is a hard part, coming up."

"Me too," said Sam. "Now I do a giraffe." He turned a page in his coloring book.

"I have to put this veal marrow—yuck; look at it—and the knucklebones into cheesecloth, and add them to the rest of the stuff. First I have to find the cheesecloth. Sam, do you know where the bandages are, the ones left over from your head last summer?"

"On my bear," said Sam. "I made him into a mummy."

"Oh, rats. Well, can I un-mummy your bear? I really need the bandages."

"Sure," said Sam agreeably.

Anastasia found Sam's teddy bear on the floor of his closet, wrapped from head to toe in gauze bandages. Only his ears stuck out. After she unwound him, she had several yards of narrow gauze. She took it back to the kitchen.

"How on earth can I wrap these bones and stuff in this gauze? You could wrap a leg, or something, but how can you wrap a whole pile of stuff like this?"

Sam shook his head. He didn't know, either.

Anastasia stared at the yards of gauze, and the mound of bones and marrow. Not even an orthopedic surgeon would be able to do this, she thought. Defeat. Utter defeat. She had gotten this far in her very first gourmet dinner, and now she was defeated by a bandage.

Finally she picked up the telephone book, leafed through the yellow pages until she found what she wanted, and dialed.

"Good Times Dance Studio," the man's voice said.

"I'm really sorry to bother you right in the middle of your tap dancing and all, Ralph," Anastasia said, "but you helped me with the corkscrew, so I thought maybe you could help me figure out how to wrap knucklebones in a long skinny bandage."

The man was silent for a moment. Then he said, "Knucklebones?"

Anastasia explained. It took quite a long time to explain, but the man was very patient.

"Geezum," he said finally, "I don't think that bandage is going to work. Lemme think. I'm thinking."

Anastasia waited.

"Pantyhose," he said finally. "Do you have pantyhose?"

"Yeah."

"Well, cut off one foot. Then you'll have like a little bag, see? And put your knucklebones and marrow into that. Then tie the top closed, with a shoelace or something. That ought to work."

Anastasia pictured it. He was right. It should

work. *"Thanks,"* she said. "You've saved my gourmet dinner."

"Well, listen, while I've got you on the phone again, how about saving my job by signing up for tap-dancing lessons?"

"Sure," said Anastasia. "Sign me up. What the heck."

She answered the questions he asked her, about her height and weight and shoe size and dancing experience. Then she hung up and went to find a pair of clean pantyhose.

By the time Anastasia had constructed the pantyhose and shoelace bag, filled it with veal marrow and knucklebones, added that to the mixture on the stove, and turned the burner to SIMMER, the washing machine was silent.

"Time to put the tablecloth in the dryer," she announced. She reached into the washing machine. "Hey, look, Sam! It really did turn purple!"

Carefully she lifted the heavy, wet, purple tablecloth and transferred it to the dryer. She turned the dryer on.

Then she looked down at herself. "Yuck," she said.

"Good thing this is a grubby old shirt. I got purple dye streaked all over it."

Sam looked over. "Your arms, too," he pointed out.

Anastasia examined her stained arms and hands. She went to the sink and washed them, but the purple remained.

"Saaaamm," she wailed. "It won't come off!"

"Like my lines," Sam said. "My purple lines don't come off, either."

Anastasia had become so accustomed to Sam's odd appearance that she had forgotten he was a road map of purple lines connecting his chicken pox spots.

"Well, you're three years old," she said irritably. "It's okay if you look stupid. But I can't be purple for my first date!"

"Wear gloves," Sam suggested.

"Like Michael Jackson?" Anastasia asked sarcastically. "That would really look terrific—about as romantic as Ringling Brothers Circus."

"No, not like Michael Jackson," Sam said patiently. "Wait a minute and I'll show you." He left the kitchen and Anastasia could hear him heading for his father's study. In a minute he was back, holding a record album. "Like this," he said, and showed her the cover.

Anastasia looked carefully at the picture of Sarah Vaughan standing beside a piano. Her hair was swept up on top of her head; she was wearing dangling earrings. And she had on gloves that went right up to her elbows.

"That looks pretty good," Anastasia mused. "Pretty sophisticated. Trouble is, I don't have any gloves like that. And Mom doesn't either."

Sam got down from his chair again and trotted off to the pantry. "Here," he said when he came back, and he handed Anastasia two quilted pot holder mittens: one blue, the other yellow with tiny red flowers.

Anastasia put one on each hand and leaned against the washing machine as if it were a piano. She struck a pose. Sam giggled.

"Caaan't help loooving that maaannnn of mine," sang Anastasia, gesturing with her thickly gloved hands.

"Good idea, Sam," she said, "but it won't work." She took the gloves off. "Tonight I'll take a bath in

Clorox. And if I'm still purple after that, I'll just make the lights very dim tomorrow night. Maybe no one will notice that I'm purple."

She found a piece of paper and a pencil. "Time for another schedule," she said.

```
              Krupnik Romantic Dinner Week Schedule

                            Version 7

Dye tablecloth.

Cook Ragout de Veau aux Champignons.

Give Sam three baking soda baths.

Try to de-purple hands and arms.

THESE THINGS WILL TAKE THE WHOLE DAY. GET DAD TO PICK
UP PIZZA FOR DINNER.
```

eight

Anastasia reached over and tapped some fish food into Frank's bowl.

"I'm sorry I forgot this morning, Frank," she said, watching him swim frantically to the surface with his mouth open. "You're a little overweight anyway, so a brief diet won't hurt."

Frank glared at her, and gulped another mouthful of food.

"I've been so busy preparing for my first date," Anastasia explained.

"And now," she went on happily, "everything's ready. I'm so well organized. I made the veal yesterday, and now it's back on the stove all ready to be heated up. And there's a gorgeous purple tablecloth on the dining room table, and two purple candles, so it's super-romantic.

"And you know what, Frank?" she asked her fish. "Dad didn't forget the flowers. He brought home a whole bouquet of purple and white chrysanthemums, and they're right in the middle of the table, and—"

She stopped talking so that she could examine herself in the mirror. Frank didn't seem to be listening anyway. Goldfish are not very good listeners.

It was five-thirty, and Anastasia was wearing her bathrobe. The Clorox bath hadn't removed all of the purple stains, but it had helped, and she would simply keep the lights very low. Her mother's makeup was waiting on the top of her desk, and laid across her bed was a dress she had found in her mother's closet. It wasn't exactly purple, but it was a deep shade of blue: close enough, especially with the dim lights.

"Anastasia?" her father called up the stairs to her third-floor bedroom.

"Yeah?"

"Have you done any laundry recently? I have a shirt to wear tonight, but it's my last clean shirt."

Anastasia made a face. Of *course* she hadn't done any laundry recently. She'd been *much* too busy with more important things. Men just didn't understand things like that.

She went down the stairs and found her father in his bedroom.

"I've gotten a little behind with the laundry, Dad," she said. "But I'm so well organized that I can put your shirts in the washing machine right now. The dinner's all made, and the table's all set, and the record is waiting on the stereo—"

"You've done a remarkable job, Anastasia," Dr. Krupnik said. "The dining room looks beautiful. By the way, I noticed that you hadn't dusted. So I just took off my shirt downstairs and ran it across the furniture."

He pointed to a pile of dirty shirts, with a dusty one on top.

"Oh. Thanks. I didn't even think about dusting. I cleaned everything up, though. I took that stack of magazines off the top of the TV, and I stuck them in the hall closet. And I picked up Sam's blocks from the living room floor, and put them behind the couch in the study." Anastasia gathered up the dirty shirts in her arms. "I'll just load these into the washing machine; then later, after the dinner party, when I'm cleaning up the dishes, I'll put them in the dryer. You know, Dad, after Mom gets home I think I can give her some lessons in organized housekeeping. It really isn't hard at all."

She took the shirts downstairs, tossed them into the machine, added detergent, and turned it on. Laundry was so easy. *Everything* about housekeeping was easy. She couldn't figure out why her mother got so frustrated.

By five minutes of seven, all three Krupniks were downstairs and waiting for the guests to arrive. They had just undergone two rather large wars.

First, Sam had refused to wear the little blue and white sailor suit that Anastasia had tried to dress him in.

"NO WAY!" Sam had screamed. "It's a baby suit! I hate it!"

"Well, it's the only good suit you have," Anastasia had pointed out angrily. "What are you going to wear if you don't wear your only good suit?"

Sam pouted. "My Incredible Hulk T-shirt," he said. "And jeans."

Anastasia glared at him. He was standing in the

middle of his bedroom wearing nothing but under-pants and a look of outrage. His whole body was a mass of chicken pox spots connected by purple lines. She wished she could hide him away in a closet and forget that he existed, just for this evening.

Instead, she tossed his Incredible Hulk shirt and his jeans to him and said, "Here, then. Put them on, if you want to look like a jerk."

Twenty minutes later she had come down from her own room, dressed for the party. Sam was sitting sullenly on his bed, still in his underpants. She ignored him.

But her father came out of his bedroom, took a look at her, and said, "No way, Anastasia. You can't come to dinner like that."

"Like what?"

He handed her a handkerchief. "Go into the bathroom this instant and remove about fourteen pounds of that makeup."

"But, *Dad*—"

"No buts. Start with the purple lipstick. Maybe you'll need to use a spatula to take off the first twelve layers."

Anastasia stomped into the bathroom and looked

in the mirror. Okay, so maybe the lipstick *was* a little thick, and dark. But *still*. Grudgingly she rubbed at it with the handkerchief.

"Can I keep the earrings on?" she yelled.

"If you want to look like Carmen Miranda, keep the earrings on," her father called.

Anastasia didn't know who Carmen Miranda was. She didn't *care* who Carmen Miranda was. She finished removing the lipstick, went back to her father's room, and tossed him the purple-smeared handkerchief. She tossed her head at the same time, so that the earrings jangled. Her father ignored her, the way she was still ignoring Sam.

Sam emerged from his room, still pouting. He was wearing jeans and the top half of the sailor suit instead of the Incredible Hulk T-shirt.

"That doesn't look too bad, Sam," Anastasia said. "You look like Popeye."

Now they were all downstairs, and suddenly it was five past seven, and just when Anastasia began to worry that neither Steve nor Annie would show up, the doorbell rang.

"You get it, Dad," Anastasia said in a panic.

"You get it, Sam," her father said, his face pale.

Finally all three of them went to the door.

"I'm starving," said Steve Harvey.

It wasn't the kind of greeting Anastasia had daydreamed about. She had envisioned someone tall and handsome—someone who looked a lot like Laurence Olivier in *Wuthering Heights*, maybe wearing a tuxedo and holding a corsage in his hand.

Steve was tall for thirteen, and he was handsome—in a braces-on-the-teeth and needing-a-haircut sort of way—but he was wearing jeans and a jacket, which he shrugged off and dropped on a hall chair. Under the jacket was the sweatshirt Steve usually wore, the one that said PSYCHOTIC STATE across the front.

"Hey, Sam," Steve said, "you look gross."

"No, I don't," Sam said. "I look like Popeye, in my sailor shirt."

"What's with the scabs?"

"Chicken pox," Sam explained.

Anastasia groaned inwardly. Would Laurence Olivier have worn a PSYCHOTIC STATE sweatshirt? Would Laurence Olivier have discussed scabs? Never. Laurence Olivier was too suave.

"And I connected my chicken poxes with Magic Markers," Sam went on, holding up one arm to show Steve.

"Please come in," Anastasia said.

"I *am* in," Steve replied. "What's for dinner? The lunch at school today was really lousy — real barf-city stuff."

"Veal," Anastasia told him. "Come on in the living room and have some hors d'oeuvres." She passed Steve the bowl of peanuts she had put on the coffee table, and averted her eyes while he stuffed a handful into his mouth. "We're expecting another guest, an old friend of my father's."

"Yeah?" said Steve with his mouth full.

"Her name is Annie O'Donnell," Dr. Krupnik explained. "She's a very interesting woman — a fine painter. She did that painting over there." He gestured toward the painting on the wall.

Steve glanced at it and grinned. "Looks like what we had for lunch today at school," he said, with his mouth still full. "I hate that kind of painting. You know the kind I like? That artist who works for *Sports Illustrated;* I forget his name. He does this great sports stuff."

"Yes, well, everyone has different taste, of course, Steve," said Anastasia's father. "I think it would be a good idea if you, ah, didn't mention to Annie that you don't care for her style. Annie's a very sensitive woman."

Steve shrugged. "Yeah, well, sure, I wouldn't tell her it looks like garbage or anything. Are there any more peanuts?"

"Sam, would you get them from the kitchen?" Anastasia asked. She was amazed. Steve had eaten the entire bowl of peanuts in two bites. Would Laurence Olivier eat peanuts like that? No way. Laurence Olivier would take one at a time, and nibble politely.

"Dad," Anastasia said suddenly, "there's a taxi out front. I think Annie's here."

And she was. She entered with a swoop, a cape flying around her, and she threw her arms around Dr. Krupnik. Her booming voice filled the high-ceilinged hall.

"Mike, you son of a gun!" Annie bellowed. "You bleeping son of a gun! Where have you been for the last umpteen years? Why didn't you ever write?"

Anastasia could see her father's startled eyes through the huge tangle of Annie's hug. No wonder he was startled, Anastasia thought. He had always described Annie as a gentle, quiet, sensitive soul—a waif with long, pale hair and a soft voice. Who on earth was this giant, booming stranger? And why was she calling him Mike? His name was Myron. Everyone called him Myron.

Dr. Krupnik extricated himself from Annie's arms and helped her take off the voluminous cape. Sam had appeared with a jar of peanuts in his hands. He stood silently and stared up at the woman. She was no smaller with the cape removed. She was enormous, both in height and width. She filled the hall. And her hair—the hair that Anastasia had heard described as long and pale—was a frizzy mass of bright red, almost orange, curls. Her eyelashes were long spikes of jet black. Monstrous earrings like doorknobs dangled from her ears, and her hands were cluttered with rings on every finger.

"I'd like you to meet my children," Dr. Krupnik said after he had hung her cape in the closet. "I'm sorry my wife is out of town.

"This is Anastasia," he said. "She's thirteen."

Annie swooped upon Anastasia. "What a bleeping horrible age, thirteen," she pronounced in her deep voice, grabbing Anastasia's hand and squashing it into the collection of rings. "Listen, kid, don't despair, thirteen doesn't last forever. Things will improve.

"Why don't you get her some bleeping contacts, Mike?" she bellowed. "You've got a kid here who looks like a bleeping *owl* with those glasses!"

"And this is Sam," Dr. Krupnik said, gesturing toward Sam, who was still clutching the jar of peanuts and staring at Annie with his mouth open.

"What does he have, premature acne?" Annie roared, laughing. She reached over and did the one thing Sam hated most in the world: she rubbed her hand through his curly hair. Sam took a step backwards. "Hey, Sambo, you're okay," she said, "even if you do have leprosy or something god-awful."

"Sam is recovering from chicken pox," Dr. Krupnik explained, but Annie didn't seem to be listening.

For Anastasia, the "Sambo" had done it. She hated Annie. She hated anyone who said "Sambo." She wished she hadn't prepared a gourmet dinner. She wished she had stuck to her plan of hot dogs, eaten standing up.

Annie had burst into the living room, where Steve was still sitting on the couch. "ANOTHER ONE?"

she brayed. "No wonder you never wrote, Mike; you spent all those years just turning out bleeping kids!"

"This is my daughter's friend, Steve Harvey," Dr. Krupnik said in a tense voice. "Steve, this is Annie O'Donnell."

Annie flung herself onto the couch beside Steve and roared with laughter. "I haven't heard that bleeping name for years!" she shrieked. "It's Annie Cummings now."

"Oh," said Anastasia's father politely. "I should have realized that you were married."

"Past tense," Annie said, and reached for some of the peanuts, which Sam had poured carefully into the bowl. "Cummings came and went, but I kept his name. Before that I was Valdez. He came and went, too. And before that was, let's see, Wolf. Or maybe it was Fox: some nasty animal, anyway."

"You've been married three times?" Anastasia asked in amazement.

"But who's counting, right?" Annie chortled. "Lemme look at you, Mike." She peered across the room at Anastasia's father. "Got a bit of a pot, and you've lost your hair. Age takes its toll, right? Look at me, I'm forty bleeping pounds overweight!" While

Anastasia watched in embarrassment, Annie grabbed two handfuls of her own stomach and shook it. She grinned. "Know what I call that? Love handles, that's what!"

Steve Harvey hadn't said a word. He hadn't even taken any more peanuts. He was simply staring. So was Sam. So was Myron Krupnik.

Anastasia took a deep breath. "Excuse me," she said. "I'm going to serve dinner."

They ate, as Anastasia had planned, by candlelight. The purple tablecloth glowed; the flowers gleamed in the center of the table. Sam sat politely, boosted up in his chair by books, and stirred the food on his plate with his fork. He picked out a few mushrooms, ate them, and left the rest.

Anastasia had lost her appetite. She ate a few bites of veal and wiped her mouth a lot with her napkin because she couldn't figure out what else to do with her hands.

Her father ate mechanically, smiling a lot, a frozen sort of smile. "It's very good, Anastasia," he said.

"Yeah," said Steve, and reached over to help himself to more.

"Good?" Annie bellowed. "It's bleeping fabulous! Did you cook this all by yourself, kid?"

Anastasia nodded.

"Well, no question," said Annie with her mouth full, "you've got a bleeping genius here, Mike. And she'll be pretty sometime, too, if she just gets rid of those bleeping glasses and quits looking like a bleeping owl!"

Anastasia stared at her plate. From the corner of her eye, she saw Annie's huge arm reach over to take another helping of veal.

Suddenly Annie screeched. "WHAT THE BLEEP IS *THIS?*"

Anastasia looked over. Annie was poking her fork at a grayish mound on her plate with a look of disgust.

"It's veal marrow and knucklebones," Anastasia said in a loud, distinct voice. "I added them to give additional flavor. That's what *Mastering the Art of French Cooking* told me to do, and it wasn't easy. It took me a long time to figure out how to do it."

"Well, you're supposed to take it *out,* kiddo, before you serve the meal. Good thing I have a strong stomach. For a minute I thought it was a bleeping dead mouse or something." Annie picked it up with a fork and spoon and dropped it back into the serving dish.

Everyone was silent. Finally Steve said, "What's for dessert?"

Dessert? Anastasia hadn't even thought about dessert. How on earth did people make dessert, too, when it took two days just to make *dinner?*

Sam looked up. "I'll serve dessert," he announced. "I'm in charge of dessert." He climbed carefully down from his chair and headed for the kitchen. In a moment he was back. He walked around the table and politely handed each person a Popsicle.

"They're grape," Sam said. "Because the color scheme is purple."

I forgot to turn on the music, Anastasia thought after Steve had left. I forgot to turn on the romantic record. With slumped shoulders she went to the kitchen and surveyed the mess. Every pot they owned was in the sink. Dirty dishes were piled on the table. Popsicle wrappings were stuck to the plates. There were spilled peanuts on the floor. The pantyhose bag of veal marrow and knucklebones lay in a sagging, soggy pile beside a cup half filled with coffee.

It was a horrible evening, she thought. Sam thought it was horrible — he had said so when she put him to bed. And Steve thought it was horrible — he had said so when she said good night to him at the door. He had also said, "Good night, Analgesia." The instant he was gone, Anastasia had run to the dictionary and looked it up before she forgot the word.

The dictionary had said, "Analgesia. Insensibility to pain."

What a lie. Anastasia was so sensitive to pain that she had been suffering the entire evening, and not just from the horrible earrings. And she was *still* suffering.

She wondered if her father thought it was a horrible evening. She couldn't tell because he had been so silent, just smiling that tense smile all through dinner.

Well, her father had *better* think it was horrible, because it was his horrible friend Annie who had made it so. She was *finally* leaving. Anastasia looked at her watch; it was almost midnight. Annie had stayed and stayed, bleating and bellowing and bleeping. Finally Dr. Krupnik had simply gone to the phone and called for a taxi. Now he was out there saying good night to Annie.

And he sure was taking his time about it, Anastasia thought angrily. At least an hour's worth of cleaning up lay ahead, and her father had promised to help with it.

She went out into the hall, and finally, after a moment, she heard the taxi door slam, and the taxi drove away. Her father came back into the house, looking exhausted.

"What took you so long?" Anastasia asked suspiciously.

"You saw what she was like," her father said irritably. "You don't think she could say good night *briefly,* do you?"

"Well, it's cold out there. You shouldn't have been out there all that time without a coat. You should have shoved her into the taxi and come back in."

Her father groaned.

"Your face is red, from the cold," Anastasia pointed out.

Then she looked more carefully. "It isn't from the cold," she said. "Your face is red because you're *blushing*, I think."

"It is not."

"It is *too*. Why are you blushing, Dad?" Anastasia wailed. "You didn't *kiss* her, did you?"

"No," he sighed. "She swooped at me, but I ducked. Maybe she kissed my shoulder. Maybe my shoulder is bright red, from her lipstick. But my face isn't red."

"Yes, it is. It's *bright red*. Come over here in the light."

Anastasia tilted a living room lampshade and examined her father's face. "Do you feel okay?" she asked.

"No," he said, "I feel lousy. I felt lousy the minute she walked in the door, and I've been feeling lousy ever since. You'd feel lousy, too, if an old friend you remembered fondly had changed that much, and turned into something so grotesque."

Anastasia touched his forehead. "You're hot," she said. "Does your head hurt? Does your nose ache? Does your bellybutton feel too tight?"

"I hurt all over."

It can't be, Anastasia thought. Please, no. But she knew. She was absolutely certain.

"Dad," she said, "guess what. You have chicken pox."

```
                   Housekeeping Schedule

                        Aftermath

Clean up. For hours and hours and hours.

Cry.
```

nine

"Mr. Fortunato," Anastasia said wearily into the phone, "this is Anastasia Krupnik. I need twenty more boxes of baking soda."

"Good grief, Anastasia, you've cleaned me out! I'll have to get them from my supplier. Let's see, today's Saturday. Can you wait till Monday for them?"

She sighed. There were still a few boxes left, and Sam didn't seem to be itching anymore. "Okay," she told the grocer. "But Monday for sure? I'll really, re-ally need them by Monday."

She turned away from the phone and looked at the kitchen, which was still in the same shape it had been in when she had left everything the night before. But worse. Now the food, which had been soggy leftovers last night, had congealed on the plates. She would have to use steel wool to get the plates clean.

And her father, of course, couldn't help. He was in bed—miserable, feverish, and complaining.

I could make up a whole new set of Seven Dwarfs, thought Anastasia: Grouchy, Itchy, Boring, Hateful, Demanding . . . It was an interesting project, but it was interrupted by the doorbell. Anastasia put down the greasy pan she was about to wash and went to the front door.

"Packages!" the mailman announced cheerfully. "Sign here."

Curiously, Anastasia signed the slip he gave her. Maybe her mother had sent some gifts from California. *That* would be nice. That would cheer her up, and take her mind off the horrible housekeeping problems. The entire bulletin board was flapping with schedules, but none of them seemed to apply to her situation now. The excitement of the dinner party was gone. Her interest in gourmet cooking was gone. Her father's availability as an adviser and helper was gone. Her interest in Steve Harvey was gone. Everything was gone except a houseful of dirty dishes, dirty laundry, dust balls under every bed, a week of untouched homework assignments, and upstairs her father calling feebly now and then for ginger ale, and announcing every five minutes that he thought he would probably die before sunset, even though the doctor had said it wasn't true.

Both packages were addressed to Anastasia, and she opened the first one, which was the larger of the two.

Sam came into the room. "What's that?" he asked, as Anastasia lifted something blue out of the box.

"I don't know," she said, puzzled. She pulled off the plastic wrapping, and exposed a blanket with some cords attached to it.

"Oh," she said, remembering something vaguely. "I guess I ordered this. It's an electric blanket. I can't remember *why* I ordered it, though."

A slip of paper fluttered to the floor, and she picked it up. She glanced at it, and her stomach lurched. She closed her eyes for a moment, hoping that when she opened them again the electric blanket would be gone and this would be a bad dream.

But when she opened her eyes, her arms were still

full of blanket and the slip of paper was still in her hand.

"Seventy-seven dollars and ninety-five cents," she read aloud in a horrified voice. "Charged to Myron Krupnik's MasterCard."

"I'm going to tell Daddy," Sam said, his eyes wide.

"No, don't. Daddy's sick. This would do him in."

She pushed the blanket back into the box and closed the lid. She stared at the other, smaller box. She tried to remember what else she had ordered.

Nothing. She had ordered nothing except groceries—she cringed, remembering the veal marrow and knucklebones—and forty-one boxes of baking soda.

Suspiciously she opened the second package and took out a bright red leotard and the ugliest pair of shoes she had ever seen in her life. They were black, with big black bows, fat heels, and metal plates on the soles.

"Wicked-witch shoes," announced Sam in awe.

"I didn't order these," Anastasia said angrily. "I know I didn't."

She picked up the paper in the box. When she saw the letterhead—GOOD TIMES DANCE STU-DIO—she cringed.

Congratulations, Anastasia Krupnik. By enrolling in our twenty-four-week tap-dancing course, you are enrolling in a future of good fun, good health, and good friends.

Enclosed is your Practix Leotard for Beginners and your special Beginner's Tap Shoes. Please bring both to your first lesson.

Since you accepted our special offer, that first lesson will be Absolutely Free!

The cost of your remaining twenty-three lessons will be our regular fee of $12.00 each, amounting to a total of $276.00.

Your Practix Leotard for Beginners cost only the special discount price of $14.95, and the Beginner's Tap Shoes, made of the finest leather, are only $24.50.

Please remit $315.45 within seven days.
WELCOME TO THE WONDERFUL WORLD OF TAP DANCING!

Across the bottom of the form letter was a handwritten note: "Hope your gourmet dinner was a success! Sincerely, Ralph." In a rage, Anastasia threw the ugly shoes across the living room, where they landed side by side in the corner by the potted azalea. She wadded up the red leotard and threw it after them. Then she kicked the box they had come in.

Sam scurried away, looking nervous.

Anastasia stomped into the dining room and pulled the purple tablecloth from the table. It was spotted with scraps of veal by Sam's place, a Popsicle puddle by Steve's place, coffee where her father had sat, and a hideous stain where Horrible Annie had held the bag of veal marrow and knucklebones suspended by her plate.

She rolled it into a ball and took it to the kitchen. Twenty-four fifty for the ugliest shoes in the world! Seventy-seven ninety-five for a stupid electric blanket!

Furiously Anastasia opened the lid of the washing machine in order to toss the tablecloth in. But something was already there. She had forgotten that she had washed all of her father's shirts the evening before. It seemed like a hundred years ago.

She reached in and pulled out the mass of damp shirts. She looked at them in horror and burst into tears. She had dyed all of her father's shirts purple.

When she had cried enough to calm down to an

occasional choking sob, she went to the desk to find the number; then she dialed her mother in California.

"There," said Katherine Krupnik with satisfaction. She held up a shirt. "Clorox is amazing, Anastasia. I don't think anyone will ever notice that those shirts have a slight purple tinge. Or if they do notice, they'll think: 'That Myron Krupnik. What a classy guy.'"

Anastasia took the shirt, hung it on a hanger, and put it with the others. "*You're* amazing, Mom. You can solve anything."

Her mother laughed. "Well, not quite. I sure didn't solve the problems with that film studio in California. It's going to be the worst animated picture ever made. I was so glad when you called and it gave me an excuse to come home."

"I felt so bad about calling you. But I thought I would probably have a nervous breakdown if I didn't. Everything in the world had gone wrong."

"I'm glad to be home. And you can go back to school tomorrow, Anastasia. Goodness, I feel terrible that you had to miss so much school!"

Anastasia shrugged. "No big deal," she said. "I can make it all up."

She looked around the spotless kitchen. It was Sunday evening, and her mother had been home only three hours. But everything was cleaned up. All of the pots and pans and plates were washed and dried and put away; they had done it together, Anastasia and her mother, and it had actually been fun.

As they were doing the dishes, Anastasia had described the horrible dinner party: the disgusting bag of veal marrow and knucklebones, the purple Popsicles for dessert, Steve Harvey and his unromantic attitude, and Annie Whatever-her-last-husband's-name-was.

"She kept saying 'bleep,' Mom," Anastasia explained. "Everything was bleeping this and bleeping that, and it was all in this horrible big booming voice. And she had frizzy orange hair, and she called Dad 'Mike'—"

"That was his nickname, when he was young," her mother explained.

"And she said I looked like an owl. And she said Sam had bleeping acne, and—" Anastasia got angry again, just thinking about it.

But her mother laughed. "Well, maybe it's a good thing. Your dad won't have fond memories of Annie anymore, and I can quit being jealous. Maybe we can even get rid of that painting. I've always hated it."

"It's gone, Mom. Dad took it down Friday night, before he went up to bed. It was his last conscious act before he collapsed with chicken pox."

Mrs. Krupnik shook her head. "Poor Dad," she said. "We'll have to be very good to him, because he feels absolutely miserable."

"Moribund," Anastasia told her. "He says he's moribund." Then she remembered something. "Mr. Fortunato's delivering twenty boxes of baking soda tomorrow," she said. "So Dad can have baking soda baths, the way Sam did. It helps the itching.

"Also," she added, with a guilty look, "we have this really neat new electric blanket."

"Nope," said her mother. "The electric blanket's going right back to the store, and I'm going to give them a piece of my mind. They should never have taken advantage of a kid your age. And you should have had more sense, Anastasia."

"I know it," Anastasia admitted.

Her mother sat down in a kitchen chair and yawned. "I'm beat," she said. "I'm going to bed. But you know what I'm going to do tomorrow?"

"Call the electric-blanket store and chew them out."

"I mean in addition to that. First I'm going to tear up the housekeeping schedule. *All* the housekeeping schedules; I notice you've made some new ones."

"Good," said Anastasia. "I'll help you tear them up. I *hate* housekeeping schedules."

"And then—" her mother began.

"I know! Then you're going to call up the Good Times Dance Studio and chew them out for taking advantage of a kid my age, right?"

"No. Then I'm going to order a microwave oven. Even though they're making a terrible movie, they did pay me a lot to act as adviser. So I'm going to buy a microwave oven. You know what a microwave oven can do?"

"No. What?"

"It thaws out frozen things. So even if I forget to thaw something out for dinner—zap! I can do it in seconds with a microwave oven."

"That solves your housekeeping problems!" Anastasia said with delight.

"Right. And *then*—"

"Then you're going to call the Good Times Dance Studio and chew them out?"

"Anastasia, let me see those tap shoes again."

Anastasia brought them to her mother. She held them out in front of her, the way you might hold something truly disgusting, with your eyes averted.

Mrs. Krupnik kicked off her own loafers and slid her feet into the tap-dancing shoes. She tied the revolting black bows.

"Mom! You wouldn't!"

Her mother stood up and tap-danced across the kitchen. *Tippety-tap, tippety-tap;* kick; twirl; *tap tap tap.* She picked up the sponge mop that was standing in the corner, held it like a cane, and circled around it, tapping. *Ta-ta TAP, ta-ta TAP.*

Then she bowed. "I'm going to do it," she said decisively. "The first lesson is absolutely free, right?"

"Right," Anastasia said, giggling. "But Mom, you *can't.* It's *gross.*"

"That may be," said her mother haughtily, "but it's fun. And it would be a break from housekeeping, which is what I need. Come on. Let's go up and visit Dad, and tell him."

Anastasia fell in behind her mother and tried to

follow the complicated hops, turns, and shuffles her mother was doing. Together they tap-danced down the hall and up the stairs. It was silly, she thought, but it was fun. And it sure felt good, having her mother back in charge.